TO: _____

FROM: _____

Wishing You A Fruitful Life!

THE *Holiday* EDITION

WOMAN! PUSH *Powerfully*

BIRTH YOUR FRUITFUL LIFE

THE *Holiday* EDITION

WOMAN! PUSH *Powerfully*

BIRTH YOUR FRUITFUL LIFE

KRISTA BARR-BASTIAN

UNIVERSAL IMPACT PRESS

Copyright © 2023 by Krista Barr-Bastian

All rights reserved.

No portion of this book may be reproduced in any form without written permission from the publisher or author, except as permitted by U.S. copyright law.

This book includes the author's personal experiences and interactions with others. While based on real events, certain details, names, and circumstances may have been altered or fictionalized to protect the privacy and identity of individuals involved. The content of this book is intended for motivation and encouragement.

While the author has shared genuine experiences and insights, readers should note that the views and opinions expressed herein are personal to the author and do not constitute medical advice, therapy, or professional counseling. Neither the author nor the publisher assumes any responsibility for any actions or decisions made by the reader based on the content of this book. While the publisher and author have used their best efforts in preparing this book, they make no representations or warranties with respect to the accuracy or completeness of the contents of this book and specifically disclaim any implied warranties of merchantability or fitness for a particular purpose.

Book Cover by Innov8 Design

ISBN: 978-1-956711-40-0

Table of Contents

Dedication	XI
Foreword	XIII
Preface	XV
Introduction	1
PUSH Principle One	14
Powerful Person	15
1. Who Are You?	17
2. My Father's Daughter	23
3. Drawing Closer	27
4. I Am Woman	35
5. I Know Who I Am!	43
Powerful Actions and Reflections	45
PUSH Principal Two	50
Powerful Purpose	51
6. Anointed and Appointed	53
7. Many Are The Plans	57
8. Where Is My Rome?	63
9. Be Fruitful and Multiply	69

10. I Know The Call On My Life!	73
Powerful Actions and Reflections	75
PUSH Principle Three	80
Powerful Presence	81
11. The Word Is Life	83
12. Faithful Promises	89
13. Set Up Your Altar	93
14. Pray Continually	97
15. I Know How To Magnify The Presence of God!	103
Powerful Actions and Reflections	107
PUSH Principle Four	112
Powerful Perspective	113
16. Out Of My Control	115
17. A Bigger Picture	121
18. Stronger, Wiser, Closer	125
19. A Necessary Sacrifice	131
20. I Have The Right Perspective	135
Powerful Actions and Reflections	137
PUSH Principle Five	142
Powerful Patience	143
21. Kairos	145
22. No Fast Track	151
23. Peace In The Wait	157
24. A Righteous Reward	161

25. I Have The Patience To Endure!	165
Powerful Actions and Reflections	167
Epilogue	173
Acknowledgments	179
About The Author	183
Holiday Edition: Exclusive Bonuses	184
Fruitful Woman Affirmation	187
Fruitful Woman Prayer	189
Fruitful Woman Scriptures	191

Dedication

This is for you! You are reading this book because God cares deeply for you. You are presently facing tough and lonely times. Life right now is overwhelming and *you feel like you are in the fight alone*. The weight of your roles and responsibilities seems just too heavy for you to bear *solo*. It's just too hard...it's just too difficult. You feel helpless and hopeless; you want to give up. But, do not be fooled because *you are not in this alone*. I want you to know that you are standing on victorious ground and I hear God saying "*Daughter, PUSH*!"

Your heavenly Father wants you to know that you were built to overcome; you are a conqueror by design. He wants you to know that *He is right beside you*. He will fight *with you*. You simply need to engage Him *by faith*. He's calling you into a *dynamic divine partnership* to birth the extraordinary amidst the chaos.

Together with God, you can claim victory in the place of your greatest challenges; in the place where you seem to be *fighting "alone"*. You can *emerge fruitfully* in that same place.

This is a call to a *partnership with God* to *transform* your *leadership*, your *influence- your life*. As you birth your *divine fruit*, the *Kingdom of God* will manifest in your sphere of influence. You are so *worthy*. You are so *necessary* to the world.

Your time is now! Fasten your faith in God and *fight* to *birth your divine fruit.*

Woman! PUSH Powerfully.

Foreword

The title of this book conjures up a most dramatic image of a woman in labour. The author captures our attention immediately, and then proceeds to teach her readers about the PUSH Principle of the *Powerful Person, Purpose, Presence, Perspective, Patienc*e, and *The Fruitful Woman Mindset*, while including prayers and Scriptures.

There is an intensity in Krista's language and an urgency in her appeal. You cannot read this book and not feel the power of God convicting and calling you to *be transformed*!

Reverend Angela Palacious, M.A., M.Div. Th.M.

FIRST FEMALE PRIEST IN THE ANGLICAN DIOCESE OF THE BAHAMAS AND THE TURKS AND CAICOS ISLANDS, COUNSELOR AND AUTHOR

Preface

I was nine months and one day pregnant and home alone with my three kids. I knew that I could be delivering at any minute. As I moved around getting prepared for the day, something happened that had never occurred in my prior three pregnancies; my water broke...on its own. *What should I do now? Does this mean that the baby is about to make his entrance now? I need help!*

I lived with my husband at the time. He took a trip off the island that morning, which left me to figure it all out *on my own*. I began frantically looking for my phone to contact my mother who lived on the next end of the island. I knew it would take her a while to get to me, especially given early morning traffic. She was the only one I thought could help me in that moment.

My effort was fruitless. I was greeted by the pre-recorded message that heightened my anxiety as it indicated that my mother's device may have been powered off. *In a moment like this? Really?* Legs wet and shaking with contractions coming in like quick subtle shocks, I called a friend who lived in my area hoping she was available to assist. *She answered! Thank God!*

She got there quickly, and we were packed and ready to go. We sat motionless in traffic as the contractions became *stronger* and *stronger*. At this point, anything seemed possible to me. Still, I hoped this baby would not make his grand entrance in her car. The ride felt like forever!

Finally, we made it to the hospital and I was wheeled in by a security officer to be checked in. The contractions became unbearable. I was in tremendous pain with *no hand to hold*. The security officer began comforting me. He was the same security officer who had greeted me excitedly two months prior when I came to pre-register at that hospital. At that time, he assured me faithfully that I would see him on my next arrival. I shrugged him off, dismissing the thought. As life would have it, he was right there *when the time came* and I needed his hand!

Completely humbled and nearly debilitated by the pain, I made it up to the room where he handed me over to the nurses who got me situated in the bed and hooked up to the monitoring devices. By this time, my doctor had arrived. She completed her necessary checks and found that I was well on my way through the dilation process, estimating at least an hour to delivery time. The contractions continued strongly and yet again with *no hand to hold*, I held unto the bed rails with a relentless grip.

It was just then, that my mother walked in. *Hallelujah!* It was like the heavens opened and shone down on me. I was both relieved and comforted to see her face. As the contractions came, two to three minutes apart, she offered her hand. After the first two grips of her hand, my nails embedding into her skin, I felt guilty. I could not share this pain with her. *I would have to bear this one alone.* She took a seat as I continued cuffing the bed rails shouting *"Jesus, Jesus!"* with every contraction.

I remember envisioning that Jesus was right at my bed side. I saw his face; I saw him reassuring me that I was *made* for this and that I had the *strength to fight* through the pain and give birth to this baby. It was *me and Jesus* through the contractions; a **_dynamic divine partnership_**.

Then came the *urge to push*. I told the nurse *it was time*. The doctor was not around but I could not wait. *With my mind still completely focused on Jesus, I began pushing!* Just then, the doctor walked into the room, in perfect time to position herself to receive the baby. I pushed powerfully through the pain, realizing that it was only there to help me birth the fruit of new life.

A few short minutes later, there he was- a healthy bouncing beautiful baby boy. I had fought through the labor pain and emerged with the *fruit of my womb*. At that very moment, I brought change to the world with the birth of a son. He was named *Kole*, and fittingly so, as his name meant *"Victory of the People"*.

I was on Kingdom agenda. This was indeed in God's plan and I executed it authoritatively because I had *absolute faith* and trust in Him. I did not discredit the pain. Though very uncomfortable, I realized it was a necessary part of the birthing process. I could not birth this fruit without a fight.

I had *no physical hand to hold* but I did have *faith in God*. This allowed me to enter *dynamic divine partnership* with Him so that <u>*I could stay focused in my mind to push strongly*</u> through every contraction that threatened to take my breath away.

I emerged fruitfully! I *partnered with Heaven* to usher a new soul to earth. This partnership led me into a higher dimension; a new version of myself. *It transformed me.* I was no longer a mother of three but of four beautiful souls. ***It happened with complete focus on God!*** Guess what? You are built to do the same!

As women, we not only have the power to overcome the pain of natural birth but also the pain of every difficult season in our lives. Once yoked with God, we have the power to fight through our hardest struggles to birth our divine fruit and ultimately be ushered into an *extraordinary version of ourselves*. A new version of you that is more impactful to the world; a *fruitful* you! This is evolution!

The more you *evolve by faith* through *partnership with God*, the more Heaven is released through you into the earth as you give birth to the will of God. This is necessary for the advancement of the *Kingdom of God* within the world. This makes you a critically important part of the mission as a *divine mother* for the *Kingdom of God*. Your *divine fruit* is necessary! You must *fight* to birth it.

This is why you are innately influential and resilient as a woman. Your unwavering faith in God makes you even more powerful. Your resilience is purified and illuminated as you continually dwell in the presence of God. There is a mental resolve afforded to you by *faith in God* that is the secret weapon of Heaven.

Less than two weeks after this birth, my husband and I separated. I was left to mother four kids <u>alone</u>: two under two. I had just left my job with the hope of finding another that would allow more flexibility as a mother of four. At this time, I strongly depended on my mother who was the most committed to walking with me as I tried to face the pain life had just dealt me. I was in despair, and it only got deeper!

Two years after this, my mother and grandmother died just over a week apart. I now felt *completely alone. Did life just leave me abandoned? Suddenly?*

Yet as disabled as I wanted to feel, God was constantly *calling me through the despair to elevation*. He did not want me to dance with the loneliness. He did not want me to pity myself in the pain. He was commanding me to transform my leadership; to realign my influence with His plans. He wanted me to fasten my *faith* in Him and *fight* my way through it until a *new* version of me emerged; a *fruitfully* version that was a complete reflection of the purposes of God in my life.

God wanted me to know that I was built so strong the struggle would have to submit to me. But I would have to take my place of authority through trusting Him; I would have to enter into the *dynamic divine partnership*.

He wanted me to understand that this trial was to be used as leverage to *push me into purpose* so I could pull out the *authenticity* which was planted deep within me. Yes, I was alone and most certainly the load was heavy but this was a call to *great transformation of my life* - transformation of my influence and my leadership which are the essence of my divine motherhood. This was a clear call to bring forth my *divine fruit*; a call I would dare to answer.

The pain gave an endless echo of the presence of greatness. The deeper the pain; the more resounding the echo became. I began to believe in the vision of greatness, to embrace it, and to become it. God wanted a *rebirth* for me and the only way to do it was for me to learn to push through this trial. I had to learn to fight with God as my divine partner through *faith*.

He wants the same for another woman. I am completely convinced that *you are her!* You are the woman God wants to emerge renewed and fruitful! *Your time is now!*

This book, *Woman PUSH Powerfully*, will show you how to fight through "life-changing" struggles and birth your *divine fruit*. It will help you to overcome in the places of responsibility where you feel *defeated; overwhelmed and alone*. It will lead you into a *dynamic divine partnership* with God so you can bring forth *divine fruit* in the very place of your struggle.

As a result of this divine birthing, you will emerge *transformed-* a brand new purposeful you! This is the victory set forth for you!

There are five powerful PUSH principles presented in this book: **Powerful Person, Powerful Purpose, Powerful Presence, Powerful Perspective** and **Powerful Patience**. These principles are foundational to a *fruitful* mindset which is necessary for *fruitful leadership and influence*. They will usher you into a dynamic divine partnership with God which is the vehicle for *divine birthing*.

If you fully engage these PUSH principles, they will fortify your *faith in God* and give you the *fortitude to fight* and spring forth anew from the trials that want to keep you entangled and barren. Your *freedom*, your *fight*, and the pathway to your *divine fruit* and *fulfillment* are in these five PUSH principles.

These principles are the pathway to your *new and fruitful life* which will only come through a fight. But, fear not! The shift in mindset that will be afforded to you by these principles will equip you for the battle. You will be readied to effectively partner with God for the "fight". Your divine fruit will come forth...YOU WILL WIN!

I see victory in your reach! I confidently declare that every part of you is enlarged and fruitful! Step into the dynamic divine partnership with God because *it is your time* to fight! It is *your time* to give birth to your *divine fruit*. Get excited, a *"new you"* is about to arise.

I see the *Kingdom of God* showing up boldly and fully in your sphere of influence; the people, places, and things under your divine leadership and mothership will come into alignment with the will of God. I see your *fruitfulness* emerging! This is your official charge, **Woman! PUSH powerfully.**

"Shall I bring to the birth, and not cause to bring forth? saith the Lord: shall I cause to bring forth and shut the womb? saith thy God." Isaiah 66:9 (KJ)

Introduction
WOMAN, WHERE IS YOUR FRUIT?

Dear Woman,

You are infinitely powerful in the purposes of God. You are deep in the struggles of life right now and you *feel alone* in facing them. I know it is heavy, but, underlying the difficulties is a crucial call of God to birth the "greater works" which He has deposited within you- *"your divine fruit".* Yes, you are pregnant!

The earth excitedly awaits your "Labor Day"- the day you release the fullness of your *divine fruit* into the earth so that the *Kingdom of God* is evident in the place under your influence and your divine mothership.

As with any birth, <u>it will not be easy</u>. *You will have to fight*. The contractions of life will attempt to strip, silence, and stifle you. But, there is still a charge for you to PUSH through it all. You will need a steadfast, unmovable faith to overcome every difficulty so that the beauty of God within you can be manifested in *your place* on the earth by way of your *divine fruit*.

You were created to manifest the glory of God. The seas flow effortlessly, the sun arises each day and sets each evening and the trees of the wild grow, bear fruit, and bring forth flowers; they are doing what they are created to do. They are manifesting the good glory of God! The same is required of us. We are being called to live in the particular purposes of God over our lives, so that God will get the glory. This is fruitfulness! *Fruitfulness does not come without a fight*; neither can you attain it without God.

Fruitfulness also begets transformation; **you cannot birth *divine fruit* and not be *transformed*.**

I want you to know that **FRUITFULNESS** requires:

DYNAMIC DIVINE PARTNERSHIP

Partnership & Obedience- God is calling you to partner with Him to do a work within the earth. This will require your absolute obedience to His word of direction. You must follow God! You must be ready and willing to walk diligently in the steps ordered by God- no matter the circumstances. This is the *dynamic divine partnership* that is founded on *faith in God*. It is the core of fruitfulness.

TRANSFORMATION

Sacrifice & Surrender- You will have to give up your personal desires including the idea of who you thought you were and accept the most *authentic* version of yourself; the identity God created you to stand in. Oddly enough, it can be very challenging and uncomfortable stepping into the "real" you, but it is critical if you are to fulfill the purposes of God. Fruitfulness will lead you to transformation as you become intentional about ensuring that *your leadership and your influence* remain aligned with the purposes of the Kingdom of God.

There is no way you can bear *divine fruit* and remain the same. Your divine fruit makes way for the emergence of a "new you" and you must be prepared to willingly relinquish the old and boldly step into your *authenticity and authority* without fear.

You may become unrecognizable to those who are familiar with you. Some of those people will be unable to understand and or accept the change in you. This is a part of the process. Do not let this hinder you. Remember you are being called to full surrender and sacrifice. You must release control and allow the authentic version of you to emerge for God's good purposes.

A transformation in you translates to transformation in the piece of the world that you lead and influence; the people, places and things that are under your divine mothership! Ultimately, your *fruitfulness* is how the *Kingdom of God* is advanced and manifested on earth through your *unique influence (*which is inspired by God through divine partnership with Him*)*.

Fruitful living will lead you to and through painful places which cannot be avoided. These are a necessary part of the process. The charge on you is to *fight*; be persistent and press your way through. This will be a sacrifice, but your steadfast faith in God will strengthen you for the PUSH! There are trials that you just cannot resist; you must go through them and overcome them to *emerge fruitfully.*

Pursuing fruitfulness can be very "messy"; it will not look or feel perfect! This is fine, *fruitfulness is not about perfection*- it is about *partnership with God* to see His will done on earth!

As you work with God for his glory, allow yourself grace. You will stumble and you may even fall but fasten your feet again and hold ever so tightly to the right hand of God. Whatever you do, do not stop walking in the steps ordered by God! *Do not stop fighting*; DO NOT STOP PUSHING!

There will be steps that may seem unbearable and unjustifiably painful, stripping you of the people and things that mattered most to you - but remember ALL things work for good! Know that God is *still* with you, and He is *still* a God of integrity. He will stay true to His every word. Trust God with it!

Get the *vision* of Heaven over the place you are in; in the roles that you occupy and PUSH until you see that vision come to full fruition- even if you are alone! Take advantage of the *dynamic divine partnership* with God and allow Him to help you *fight to birth* your *divine fruit*. Your *divine fruit* has an appointed time. Always remember to be patient; master the disciple of waiting as you trust the perfect timing of God.

I want to reiterate; walking into your fruitfulness *is not easy*. The process of birthing your divine fruit is far from pretty or perfect- I really need you to understand this. But your greatest power is the presence of God, so engage Him through the Holy Spirit. *You are not alone*- God is with you right here, right now!

I do not know the particulars of your trials and troubles but with God you can overcome and emerge with your *divine fruit*. You may be alone in the natural but a *dynamic divine partnership* with God gives you access to divine resources that afford you an extraordinary advantage in the fight so that you PUSH with power.

As humans, we all have some level of trials and disruptions- we all must endure and overcome. Writing this book was a huge feat for me. I knew God required this of me. I knew this was my *divine fruit* so I believed that it would *transform me* and *transform the world around me*. But, I did not want to write this book until I found myself perfectly at the "top of the mountain"; at the place of promise.

However, God kept urging me to do it now, right here in the "pit" where things were still chaotic and a complete mess.

I found myself "doing" life *alone* as a single-separated mother of four kids as a result of a broken marriage. This was compounded by the challenge to adjust to the deaths of both my mother and grandmother which happened nine days apart and closely followed my separation. *Life was heavy and lonely.* Yet still, I had to do the work God was calling me to; I had to PUSH to birth my *divine fruit.* I had to be obedient irrespective of my circumstances and work to get this message out.

You will not have the option to wait for things to "get right" before you begin to work. You have got to learn to work in the "mess" and engage the presence of God as you work. This is the *fighting spirit* that comes through *dynamic divine partnership* with God which is necessary for *fruitfulness.*

Many times, I was alone, discouraged, and bewildered. You may be feeling that same way right now. You may be weary and your desire to PUSH may be gone. In times like these, I would find comfort and inspiration in the Old Testament story of Joseph and his most challenging path to being positioned in the ultimate purposes of God. God led him to be fruitful in the place of his greatest suffering.

I encourage you to take a read of his story in the book of Genesis 39-41 and I pray that you find strength and comfort there as well. The God of Joseph is still alive today! Allow Him to be your God through *dynamic divine partnership* and see your *fruitfulness* emerge.

It was not until the completion of this book that I realized it was not only written for you, but it was also written for me! I am still very much in the process of "pushing" and *divine birthing.* I am still *"fighting for my fruit".* When I get discouraged, I also return to the pages of this book for inspiration and strength to PUSH.

You will come to understand that "pushing" is a lifestyle. As long as you are breathing, you are expected to be engaged in birthing fruit. As women, we are in a perpetual state of birthing and evolving. So, "pushing" is more of a marathon than a sprint. There is a constant call on you to overcome the hurdles and endure the valleys until the full vision of your fruitfulness shows up in earth. *You are not done fighting until you SEE the fullness of your divine fruits with your natural eyes.*

Always remember, it is your fruitfulness that God desires the most from you! As long as you are alive, God requires you to be fruitful in whatever place, position or role you are in. One of God's first commands to the man and woman upon creation was "Be fruitful and multiply." (Genesis 1:28). This goes beyond just natural procreation. I do believe that God was urging the man and woman to do what he created them to do; to find and operate according to their particular purposes of God. This means walking in obedience to His word over your life- *no matter the circumstances!* Then and only then will you come to a place of fulfillment because you have satisfied the purpose for which you were created.

God found David, the great warrior King of the Old Testament, to be a man after his own heart. David did whatsoever God required of him. Will you be a woman after God's heart today? God is calling you to *listen more closely to His voice* and to *follow Him*. He has a word concerning you, *will you draw closer to Him?*

Your Creator, who is also your Heavenly Father, has a piercing question for you today. He is asking **"Woman, where is your fruit?"** God is looking for a new breed of women that are passionate about their fruitfulness. We are currently facing a motherhood crisis. Women are showing up fruitless in the earth.

We are being consumed by the contractions and distractions of life thereby neglecting our chief responsibility of birthing our *divine fruit*. But, no more! I am here to help you PUSH to birth your divine fruit for your transformation and the transformation of the world around you so that the mission of the *Kingdom of God* continues to be advanced.

Every woman, irrespective of whether she bears a child in the natural, is a "mother". She has the ability to lead, influence, and mold the environments in which she occupies. This influence gives birth to her *divine fruit*. As a woman, you are critically important to the *Kingdom of God* at this time. You are the fertile ground necessary for God's purposes to sprout in the earth. Heaven needs you to fight for your fruit! Heaven needs you to **PUSH...NOW!**

I want you to know that I understand the challenges. As a woman faced with a lot of struggles, I recognize that it is not easy!

You are overwhelmed and tired; battered by it all. Life is coming up against you strong and hard. You may even feel like the magnitude of the difficulties is not justified- you don't deserve this.

Your feelings are valid but you must rise above them. You cannot stay stagnant and entangled by your emotions. *Give it to God and get on pushing.* We as women are in the fight of our lives to birth our *divine fruit* to preserve and proposer the world around us. Our *divine fruit* is the light the world needs.

If we refuse to fight to bring our fruit forth darkness will wreak havoc among us. We have got to commit to the **<u>fight to birth our fruit</u>**. We truly have no option; **WE MUST FIGHT! WE MUST FIGHT NOW!**

The enemy understands the importance of your *divine fruit* and *the redemptive power attached to it.* He will do everything to block you from birthing it; hitting you from every angle of life.

There is a full attack on the woman. From the beginning of time, there was a mandate to deceive woman and ultimately destroy mankind. The first deception happened with Eve in the Garden of Eden where the serpent deceived her into eating the forbidden fruit. God then placed enmity between the woman and the serpent; between her seed (fruit) and his seed (Genesis 3:15).

Satan still wants to distort your vision today! He wants to steal and destroy your fruitful vision so it does not manifest in the world. He wants to keep you barren. Woman, you must no longer be distracted and deceived! Get the vision of God over the places and people that you influence; this is your picture of fruitfulness. Protect and preserve your vision with passion and pursue it in *partnership with God*!

It was a fruit that caused the ultimate fall of mankind but it will be the divine fruit of women that protects, preserves, and prospers the earth and everything in it. This is why there is redemptive power in your fruit! Do not allow Satan to continue to deceive you about your identity and authority and distract you with life's difficulties.

You must fight back! Keep your vision pure and BIRTH YOUR DIVINE FRUIT! Victory is in the birth of your *divine fruit*!

While the fight is necessary to bring forth your fruit, remember *you should not fight alone*. Step into a *dynamic divine partnership* with God. Refuse to allow the trials to keep you weak and barren. *You are a fruitful woman!* Come out of the struggle with *divine fruit* that will *crush the head of the enemy*! **THIS IS WAR**- and you are a worthy opponent. As a citizen of the Kingdom of God, victory is your name; it is your birthright so claim it.

GOD IS CALLING YOU TO MAKE YOUR INFLUENCE PURE! He is calling you to bring forth *divine fruit*. It is your consistent prayer and communion with God that will allow this to happen. This allows for a *dynamic divine partnership* with God that will enrich the earth and advance the Kingdom of God.

Once you are persistent in your partnership with God the world around you and everything attached to you must step into alignment with the will of God- there is no option- it is a must! You are a keeper called to cultivate everything under your influence in accordance with the good will of God!

You are a fighter called to protect and preserve everything under your care! You are a fruitful woman called to birth Heaven into your space on earth!

Are you petitioning Heaven for the welfare of your homes, communities, and by extension your country? Women must carry a sensitivity to the spaces in which they are in. When those spaces become misaligned with the will of God, it must grieve the hearts of women and draw us to God in prayer for its restoration and preservation.

This is what *fighting* is about! You must fight for your *divine fruit* to show up in the places and spaces you occupy and influence. Your fruit is representative of your godly influence and therefore it should be in alignment with the will and good purposes of Heaven.

You are a great woman of God- a *"Kingdom Mother"*. Heaven needs you to step into your rightful authority! Heaven needs you to fight for your *divine fruit*! It is the godly values by which you will raise your children, counsel your husbands, build your businesses and ministries, and encourage your brothers and sisters that will make a difference for generations to come; building a great legacy of faith and fruitfulness.

God is looking for you to help shift the trajectory of the world. He is looking for you to help promote and restore the principle of *faith in God* in the world. There are people, places, and platforms attached to your influence; your spiritual womb. God is calling you to cultivate, lead, and "mother" them *by faith. This is fruitfulness!* He is not asking you to do it alone. He is your help through a *dynamic divine partnership!*

Woman, are you ready to transform and be transformed? Heaven is excited that you are here! This is where God wants you. Every word on every page of this book has been scribed just for you. I beg of you, at the end of your life, do not allow God to ask you the most dreaded question *"Woman, where is your fruit?"*

I am here to help you establish the *fruitful mindset* necessary for the *fight of divine birthing* so that you can avoid this- please allow me to do so. Commit yourself to reading the pages of this book intentionally and prayerfully. Ask the Holy Spirit to expound the pages of this book; to open it up deep and wide thereby bringing immense revelation concerning your identity and your authority to birth divine fruit.

Begin with a firm expectation that you will be equipped with the fortitude of mind to fight fiercely as you look to step into the *fullness of your fruitfulness.*

Welcome to your labor room! You are about to step into five powerful PUSH principles that will help you fortify your mind and usher you into a *dynamic divine partnership* with God so you can birth your *divine fruit*. These will be necessary for your fight to emerge fruitfully:

Powerful Person- The understanding that you were created in the image and likeness of God. You are a ruler! You are also woman, made with the innate ability to influence, transform, and keep the spaces in which you are placed in alignment with the will of God.

Powerful Purpose- You are here to serve a people, a people that are waiting to be "delivered" by your divine fruit. God has set you apart to birth a particular "work" into this earth. You need the vision of your assignment.It is this vision that is the start of your fruitfulness.

Powerful Presence- You are to create an environment that will magnify the presence of God around you. Dwell in the scriptures of God, constant prayer and praise, and remaining mindful of His promises toward you, support and strengthen you on the journey toward fruitfulness.

Powerful Perspective- You must be persuaded that every trial is a necessary sacrifice that you must endure to birth your divine fruit on earth. The trials, the struggles, the challenges, and the pits are not personal instead they are purposeful!

Powerful Patience – You will birth your divine fruit and come to your promise in the appointed time of God. He makes everything beautiful in its time. There is a time attached to your fruitfulness. Don't get weary in birthing! Allow time to properly position you for fruitfulness. Continue to endure and PUSH! It will happen at *Kairos*, the appointed time of God.

BARR-BASTIAN

Fruitful woman, this is your birthing season. *Bring forth your divine fruit!...* you have full permission to PUSH!

Your Sister in Fruitfulness,

KBB

Krista Barr-Bastian

Woman! PUSH Powerfully, Author

> "But that on the good ground are they, which in an honest and good heart, having heard the word, keep it, and bring forth fruit with patience" LUKE 8:15

PUSH PRINCIPLE
ONE

POWERFUL
Person

CHAPTER 1

Who Are You?

In order to emerge from the difficult places in your life with your divine fruit, *you must know who you are.* Knowing your true identity in Christ is critical to pushing powerfully through the tough times. It is your confidence in your true identity that will help you to fortify your faith and establish effective partnership with God as you *fight to birth your divine fruit.* Let's uncover the truth about your identity as a creation of God, His daughter and the specifications of your design as a woman.

It is accepted, if not expected, of you to identify yourself in some manner when you are first introduced to someone unfamiliar. As humans, we have an insatiable desire to know about each person we engage with. This is a completely reasonable norm because this is how we make decisions about who we choose to further connect with. However, the bigger part of this is that many of us really have no idea who we are. Our identification of ourselves is typically very worldly and this is usually because these are the aspects of ourselves that are most obvious to us.

Think about it, if someone approaches you with the million-dollar question *"Who are you?"* what is your first response? We normally default to telling them our names, we may proudly boast of our occupation, quickly announce our marital status, enthrall them with our latest accomplishment or even walk them through the joys of parenthood.

Whether you've been a top-selling sales manager for thirty consecutive years or a mother for two decades or even a swimmer since birth, I want you to know that none of this is who you are.

I am a single mother of four by separation, a former Certified Public Accountant, and due to the tremendously difficult season I have had to overcome, I also consider myself a life-certified fighter. My travels here, to this very point of my life, had me feeling quite like Sofia from the movie *The Color Purple* whose famous line was *"All my life I had to fight!"* While this may sound interesting; this is not who I am! Not even your sorrow can frame you because it only lasts a season. *Thank You Jesus!*

Memories are so precious; my mother is no longer here with me, but she continuously challenged me to embrace the truth of me beyond the facades.

During my senior year of high school, I decided to attend senior prom at the very last minute. I had no date and really didn't have time to appoint a glam squad to design the "perfect look" worthy of the grand entrance that is normally expected at proms.

I had borrowed a dress from my aunt, shoes from another aunt, and one of my cousins did my hair and make-up. I was ready for my 2002 senior prom and jumped into my mother's 1992 champagne Toyota Camry. The car was not cleaned, and my mother served as my driver with a complete roller set in her hair. This was fine with me because the hotel hosting us had a main entrance at its lower level and a secluded entrance on the upper level. My plan was to slip through the quieter entrance above, while everyone else was making a spectacle down at the front entrance.

As we approached the hotel, I could see a crowd of spectators lined up at the main entrance to welcome my classmates and their dates. At this point, I began beckoning to my mother to drive up to the next entrance and, she refuses. She joins the line for the main entrance and begins to lecture me on the importance of my identity. Just then a vehicle pulls up behind us and now there is no way out. Here is her dusty Camry parked between two sparkling white limousines and the only thing I can hear her say is, *"You are Krista Barr, and no one can change that."*

It sounded good and I knew she wanted to instill something powerful within me but at that age there was too much at stake. I needed to protect my image and avoid complete embarrassment. I left my mom lecturing as I exited her car anxiously and in such a panic to fix this situation that I did not even say good-bye. Next thing I knew, I was knocking on the window of the limousine directly in front of us, not knowing who was on the inside. They allowed me in where I met two couples waiting to make their grand entrance. We were up next, so I quickly took control and asked the first couple to exit, then turned to the second couple and asked that they follow behind me.

Clearly, I had no confidence in who I was! I was completely convinced that a prom entrance would define me. From that day, all the way until now, I have never forgotten the words of my mother whenever life threatens to assign a false identity to me. *I am Krista Barr and NO one or NO situation has the authority to change that!*

I want you to know that there is certainty in your identity. Therefore, your identity does not change with circumstance. *It is stable and it is constant.* Your occupation, your place of residence, your citizenship, your marital status, your possessions, and your interests can all change from season to season.

But your identity, the core of you, never changes. It stays firmly grounded irrespective of the changes in your life. When you are now wanting to identify yourself with something that is constant, we are led to take it all the way back to the first days; in the beginning where it all started. As people of faith, we know that our creative process began in the Garden of Eden thousands of years ago.

Genesis 1:26-27 takes us into the exact thought of God as He prepared to give life to the pinnacle of creation, the human being. This is His blueprint, and it reads: *"And God said, Let us make man in our image, after our likeness: and let them have dominion over the fish of the sea, and over the fowl of the air, and over the cattle, and over all the earth, and over every creeping thing that creepeth upon the earth. So, God created man in his own image, in the image of God created he him; male and female created he them."*

There you have it! This fits the certainty criteria. Your identity is grounded in the likeness and image of God. This is the very fiber of you, and it cannot change. You are created to think like God does and therefore to act in the ways of God to some extent.

He calls you *Ruler*, which is what He does. He rules sovereignly over the heavens and earth. He has created you, as human, to dominate over all other living creatures in the earth. He has made you with a likeness that allows rulership to be possible! He has given you a presence of power and a capacity of mind to reign with authority in the earth. You are created to have a mind like Christ. You are fully loaded! This is a constant capacity that cannot change. You have had access to it since the day you were conceived and still it's available to you today.

I want you to arise from wherever you are right now and run to a place where you can see your reflection, whether that be a mirror, the glass of a store front or even the windows of a nearby vehicle. *Pause!* Take a good long look at yourself and declare these words, *"I am a Ruler!"* Whether or not you are showing up or feeling like the ruler you are doesn't negate the fact that you were created for it!

Now that we've made it abundantly clear that you are more than your daily roles, you are empowered to embrace and experience the truth of your identity. There should be a burning desire within you to go deeper. To dig beyond the surface of your daily roles and the variables of the equation of life and to find the constant; *the true glory of God rooted securely within you.*

So, allow me to first introduce myself, I am a living being made by God in His very image and likeness. I have the power of mind that affords me the authority to rule over all other living creatures of the earth. Birds fly and fish swim, however, I, by the power of my mind through the authority delegated to me by God, rule!

Yes, I am a Ruler! Who are you?

Chapter 2
My Father's Daughter

You are your father's daughter! You are made in his image and likeness to rule with power and authority! As with any parent and child relationship, there is a likeness involved- not only because there is a great deal of time spent together but also because there are innate commonalities; they share the same biological make up.

It is quite the same here with you and the Heavenly Father. A child can almost always see themselves in their parents especially as they begin to age, and most parents often start to see themselves being reflected in their children as well. I have mothered four children and I see myself showing up in each of them in different ways. The older I become, I notice a great deal of the mannerisms of my parents springing up in me also. *We are mirrors*. We reflect the prestige and the honor of our fathers. We carry the legacy of our fathers and are true representations of them. God wants the same thing to be shown within us. He wants our ways, and our actions to clearly reflect everything that represents Him as our Heavenly Father.

We as humans are most complex in our makeup. We are first spirits with a soul, encapsulated in an earthly body. If we are after perfecting the likeness of God as He so created us to, then we are required to do this from our spirits.

Because God, our creator and Father is a Spirit, to show up in His likeness as ruler we are required to increase in our spirit. We live in an earthly realm which is highly physical and compels us to operate and respond from our natural senses which are trigged by our earthly interactions. Therefore, most of the time we are unable to tap into the truth of who we are as rulers because the capacity to do so is poured out from our spirit; our internal not our external. This is the place where God and I, Father and Daughter can commune freely in full understanding. This is the place where I mirror my father, where I show up in my representation. This is the place where the *dynamic divine partnership* between Father and Daughter is built. This is the place of beauty and a complete joy for a Father to witness His daughter digging deep to display the identity of the royal lineage, as she seeks to carry the legacy with a posture of excellence and authority.

To know your father is to take on the same mindset of your father. The world has had a chance to see this clearly displayed in the lives of the late *Kobe Bryant* and the late *Gianna Bryant*. Bryant was a very well-known American professional basketball player. During his 20-year career, he built a legacy that the world could not deny. His discipline and dedication to the sport led to records and accolades that still stand present even in his absence from the world. Kobe was a father to four beautiful daughters and, with a legacy like his, I can only imagine that there was a desire to birth a son that could carry it forward for generations to come.

He did not have a son, but he did have a *determined daughter*. A daughter who knew her father. She knew he possessed a top tier mindset and skillset. She saw the greatness of her father and was completely convinced that somewhere deep within her she had it too because she came from him. He was the cloth that she was cut from. She identified herself with him and stayed close to him because she believed that his basketball talent was also present in her. Gianna Bryant confidently offered herself up to be trained by her father to carry on the legacy. Kobe, intrigued by her willingness, opened himself up and poured into her. Consequently, he began to see the beauty of his legacy spring forth through her.

When you want to know who you are, you must start at the root. The root will tell you all about the shoot and its fruit. Gianna knew she came from a great root and, with her being the shoot, she was convinced that greatness existed in her as well. She was determined to dig deep and bring it out. She was completely persuaded about her capacity to perform on the level of her father because she believed that she carried his likeness. While the world may have considered Kobe's legacy dead in the absence of a son, Gianna- a daughter, stood up as a child made in his image and asserted her ability to encapsulate the greatness of her father. At the tender age of thirteen, she had already begun to make great strides in the game of basketball. Their unfortunate demise truly broke the hearts of sports fans worldwide. However, their relationship and likeness continues to resonate deeply as it has brought light to the wonder of a strong father-daughter relationship.

Like Gianna, you are a daughter. Your father is calling you to realize the innate capacity you carry to show up *like Him* in the world. You must be completely persuaded about this and be intent on unlocking it. In Jeremiah 33:3 Christ urges us *"Call unto me, and I will answer thee, and show thee great and mighty things, which thou knowest not."* God reveals himself through intimate relationship with you which flows from earnestly seeking Him. *Daughter*, then and only then will you reflect the grandiose glory of your father.

You are the daughter of a great Father. Think of any individual that you hold in high esteem because of their accomplishments, accolades, or authority in a certain area. Know that your father is far greater than this! He is the creator and sovereign ruler of the earth and the heavens and you my dear, yes you, are His daughter! You were made in His great image, fashioned to exhibit the magnificence of who He is.

Can you even begin to imagine the magnitude of the power of who you are, merely because you are the daughter of the Heavenly Father? Like Gianna, activating this power simply *requires your faith*. You must *believe*, that because of the blueprint of your creation, you can show up majestically like your heavenly Father.

You are royal!

So, put on your crown daughter, *rule and reign*...just like your Father!

Chapter 3
Drawing Closer

To release the power of who you truly are you must draw closer to the source. There is an intimacy that is required for you to unlock the innate power in you to be what God has created you to be, *a ruler*. This is in alignment with the scripture of James 4:8 which affirms this fact, stating *"Draw nigh to God, and he will draw nigh to you."*

For there to be an awakening of the beauty of you there must be an alignment with God. You cannot show up in your true divine identity until you are aligned, until you have opened your spirit to receive what God wants you to download so that you activate your authenticity. This is a critical part of posturing yourself for the push. Your capacity to birth your *divine fruit* is hinged significantly on your ability to unlock the truth of your divine design.

This activation is foundational to your fruitfulness and requires you to change your mindset; to renew your thinking. It is your mindset that becomes the channel for your connection with God through the Holy Spirit. Your renewed mindset: your new way of thinking and believing as a result of drawing closer to God, gives you access to the fullness of authority available and accessible to every human being that *wills* it. Romans 12:2 reminds us that we are transformed by the renewing of our minds.

This book is a call to shift your mindset through the engagement of the push principles of *divine birthing* so that you can step into your *fruitful transformation*. Hence, transformation begins with words; ideas and thoughts that shift your belief and ultimately your behavior.

John 1:1 states, *"In the beginning was the Word and the Word was with God, and the Word was God."* The incorruptible word of God, which is himself, is where you start. Jesus says in John 6:63 *"The words that I speak unto you, they are spirit, and they are life."* He also asserts in Mathew 4:4 that *"Man shall not live by bread alone, but by every word that proceedeth out of the mouth of God."*

The word of God is therefore necessary to live life in the likeness and the image of God. Remember, you are transformed by the renewing of your mind; the words that you dwell in transform you. So, meditation in the scriptures will transform you. You will begin showing up in the likeness of God- with a divine boldness and authority. This is exactly the spirit you need to fight through the chaos of life and birth your *divine fruit*.

There is a requirement for you to develop an appetite for the scriptures. Take time to renew your mind with the scriptures so that you can discern the word from heaven as it is revealed. There is a new comprehension of your identity that is cultivated through studying the scriptures that cannot be garnered or ascertained by merely transacting physically on the earth. This is the first and most critical step to learning about the true power of you. You must have a desire to become fully acquainted with the word of scripture- this is imperative for fruitfulness.

It takes a great deal of personal commitment to get close to God. For many of us the practice is quite unfamiliar. We are not in the habit of entering a daily, intense, study of the word. We dare to live daily on the little bit of *"hand-me-down"* faith passed on by our grandmothers and mothers. We fail to step into the fullness of who we are in Christ because we neglect seeking Him for ourselves.

This intimacy with God requires isolation. It requires you to remove yourself from common spaces and create an atmosphere that is heavily focused on God. This is where God gets your complete undivided attention. This is an extreme level of commitment, and it only can be birth from a pure desire to know God and ultimately know more of you. This is where a *dynamic divine partnership* takes root.

I've had the privilege to read books and listen to numerous sermons by the late *Dr. Myles E. Munroe*, a man who has profound wisdom in Kingdom leadership and purpose. He spoke often about finding authentic power by engaging the scriptures which he refers to as the *"owner's manual"*. This is where you will find the ultimate revelation to empower you. I have proven this to be the full truth. Immersion in the scriptures of God will give you a greater understanding of your identity and your authority.

Dr. Munroe often proudly boasted that he became powerful in his tender teen years, at which time, he had read the entire bible and came to an understanding of his authority as a child of God. He had a confidence that the world could not shake because of his intimacy with the scriptures. It is this confidence that gives you the tenacity to push powerfully through life and *birth your divine fruit*.

God, through scriptures, has an impact on your mind- the way you perceive yourself in relation to your life's circumstances. As a result, you will carry a bold, fearless, and courageous mindset; allowing you to stand resiliently against the blows of life.

This is why it is so important to protect your mind. It should be treated as a private space. Be very particular about who and what you allow to sit with you there. It determines how you show up in your life! Proverbs 4:23 states *"Keep thy heart with all diligence; for out of it are the issues of life."* Mind and heart can be used interchangeably here. Your mind ultimately directs the affairs of your life. Therefore, you must keep it in the presence of God for peace, prosperity, and fruitfulness.

Spending time with God transforms your thinking. You begin to think more on a heavenly level. You begin to adopt the mindset of God as the Holy Spirit is given free rein to govern and direct your thoughts according to the way of God. Two like mindsets can relate; two like mindsets can communicate. Thus, you will be able to connect and receive from God as you have now created a channel that can facilitate a *dynamic divine partnership* to support you as you *birth your divine fruit*.

You will be able to identify the voice of God and follow His lead simply because you have formed an intimate relationship with Him. John 10:14, 5 Jesus says *"I am the good shepherd, and know my sheep, and am known of mine... And a stranger will they not follow, but will flee from him: for they know not the voice of strangers."* Do you know God so well that you can clearly hear and recognize his voice in your life? *Are you close enough?*

My spiritual journey started with the word of God. I remember wanting so badly to truly live a powerful and *fruitful* life. There was a calling within me to go deeper, a calling that told me that so much more was required of me. It compelled me to engage with the word.

We all have it. We all have the yearning and desire for deep fulfillment and the only way it is truly satisfied is by feeding on the word. It is a call to get to know the higher fruitful version of who we are. Many times, we misunderstand the desire and attempt to satisfy it on our own with the devices of the world to no avail.

The imperishable, incorruptible, word of God is the only key that will unlock the truth of who you are and ultimately bring the fruitfulness and fulfillment you desire. The scriptures are core to your engagement and partnership with God. It is through scripture that He reveals dimensions of himself (and yourself) to you through His Holy Spirit. This revelation is essential as you seek to partner with God to overcome the difficulties before you and emerge to lead a *fruitful* life.

It was God that led me to desperately seek Him through the word. I was newly separated from my husband with four young kids and just completely heartbroken; totally shattered. Just a few months later, I was led to the door of the next valley, to which I responded with an emphatic *"No!"* I knew this place. I had been here before. This is only pain and damage. Yet, God urged me to *walk* through it. It was a path I had to take.

I didn't understand it. I didn't understand why God would opt to lead me through the dreary dark way instead of a "scenic route". I was fresh out of a chaotic and troubling season, and in my mind, I needed a break. I believed that I now deserved the quickest, easiest, prettiest path to stepping into my fullness and fruitfulness.

However, God knew that the pain and pure confusion of this new situation would quickly amplify my desire to get closer to Him, and that it did. I lived in the word. I clung to God, and everything that had anything to do with Him, like never before. Consequently, I grew by leaps and bounds. My dwelling in the word of God became evident through the *divine fruit* which began springing forth from my life; this book is a part of that harvest.

Get closer! Devotionals are a great place to get started. Sarah Young's *"Jesus Calling"* is a wonderful collection of effective devotionals to help you begin your walk with God. Also, ensure that you own a bible. If you do not have a personal copy go and purchase one. A bible study group is a great way to get started. If you cannot find one, create one!

As you become more and more immersed in the word you will find that a hunger will develop. You may quickly see yourself transitioning from group study to self-study. Once you begin to dive and dwell in the word alone, you give way for an intimacy to be created with Heaven that is favored in the eyes of your Father. He then reveals some of the mysteries of who you are and all things concerning you. Do all that you possibly can to passionately pursue a relationship with God. It is *necessary* for fruitfulness and fulfillment.

Prayer is also a critical part of this process. God loves when we initiate fellowship and communion with Him. This signals to Him that we want more of Him as we are relentless in our seeking. Knowing more of who He is leads to more of a revelation of who we are. Having conversations with God through prayer creates a relationship necessary to receive Him as Father, the all-knowing and powerful ruler of the earth and the heavens.

Again, this is the basis of the *dynamic divine partnership* with God which allows for communication that is primary to your fruitfulness. Do not be intimated by prayer. Always remember. God is not requiring eloquence He just wants purity of heart. Pour out to him in your own simple way. Most importantly, *listen intently for His response*. Prayer is a dialogue between you and God; keep the two airways of communication open.

Both study and prayer are most powerful when done simply and sincerely. What is required most of all is a heart that is sincerely postured, purely wanting to know God and wanting Him to open up and receive you.

This is also a very humbling act. You are presenting yourself to Him as a branch of His tree wanting to be fully initiated under His order. You are not seeking to make an identity for yourself, but you recognize that you are a derivative of Him; you are from Him.

You know Him to be the *only* way to the most authentic version of you. You are presenting yourself for service; you want to *partner* with God and participate in the plans of His Kingdom that concerned you from the day of your conception. The very plans that gave you divine purpose in this life; the plans that gave you your intricate identity and divine authority.

It is important to note that you are not unlocking your authenticity just for your own benefit. I want you to know that the identity you decide to live in today influences the identity of your children and the generations that follow them. Wherever there is influence there is leadership. You will be held accountable for your leadership. This is why it so important to make every effort to get it right.

Hence, it is your duty and obligation to set the foundation and leave an inheritance of true identity based on *faith in God*. This creates a covenant of prosperity for generations that will only have the privilege of being told about you.

You do this by drawing closer, right now. What you do now impacts generations ahead. There is a high call on you to be responsible with your identity and influence. Create an environment; people, places, and things that surround you with the word.

Always aim to keep the presence of God in your space. Continuously draw yourself close; that's intimacy. Intimacy will get you to know who He is and will give you confidence about who you are in Him.

Intimacy is the foundation of a *dynamic divine partnership* which is necessary for you to live on purpose and birth the divine fruit of your calling right where you are.

CHAPTER 4
I Am Woman

You are not only a creation of God, but what's also completely special about you is that you are a woman. As a woman, there are intricate details about you that make you different from a man. God created you as a ruler as he did man. This is evident in Genesis 1:27 where he states, "So God created man *in his own image, in the image of God* created he him; male and female created he them." You were created in the image of God to be powerful by your spirit.

Eve was the prototype of creation for the woman. She was intended to represent how a woman should function or be effective in the space or environment in which she was positioned. God's idea to create Eve came before Adam knew there was even a need for her.

Genesis 2:18 states, "It is not good that the man should be alone; I will make *him* a help meet for *him*." The creative process is outlined in Genesis 2:22 which states "And the rib, which the Lord God had taken from man, made he a woman, and *brought her unto the man*."

Adam's response brings in another dimension to the creation and identity of the woman. Genesis 2:23 states "And Adam said, this is now bone of my bones, and flesh of my flesh: *she shall be called Woman*, because *she was taken out of Man*." This would therefore suggest that not only is woman a derivative of her father God, but she is also a derivative of man. She mirrors him in some aspect. She finds her innate power of rulership through God and finds her specific domain of influence with man. Hence, her leadership and the fruitfulness thereof is attached to a man. He is the identification of her specific sphere of influence which is to be done in *partnership with God*.

We see this, particularly with mothers who are responsible for raising the children that they bear with a man. God is expecting that they raise their children under godly influence thereby producing faithful servants for the Kingdom of God- this is fruitfulness.

This is why it is critically important for a woman to step into her authentic identity in God. Genesis 2:21 notes "And the Lord God caused a *deep sleep* to fall upon Adam, and he slept." There are a lot of men still *"sleeping"* today. They are living outside of their natural God-given authority. They are not connected to who they were created to be. Consequently, God is unable to work through them.

This cannot be an excuse for women to slack and slumber as well. If we as woman are mirrors, then, it is imperative that we become serious about the pursuit of the truth of our identity so that the men around us will connect with their authenticity (as Adam saw a reflection of himself in Eve - Genesis 2:23) and ultimately be awaken from their slumber.

We must remember that we are partners with God. It is not our duty as women to work to change a man for our personal pleasure, please understand that we must always be on God's agenda. God is multifaceted and strategic. Your role in the places you are positioned is so much bigger than you. It is an obligation of ours to seek and occupy the space of our authenticity in God; so that we can be great partners of the will of God. When we do this, everything that we are connected and attached in the earth to must take its rightful position for the accomplishment of God's will, including men.

God engaged us in the earth's work as helpers. Above all other things, this requires us to prioritize and purify our partnership with God. We cannot be good helpers if we do not have a good partnership with the God who designed and deployed us for His work.

This is why the *dynamic divine partnership* with God is entirely important to your fruitfulness as a woman; *a heaven-sent helper.* The advancement of the Kingdom of God comes through your womb in the form of your divine fruit. Your fruit is the result of your influence. Your influence is the execution of the will of Heaven concerning the place you are put in. This is how you help; you ensure that your influence over the people, places, and things attached to you is aligned with the desire and plan of God.

God intended for man and woman to walk together to rule in the earth in their specific spheres of dominance (Genesis 1:27-28). The woman's authenticity and divine influence over a man is critical in this. This is clearly evident in Genesis 3: 12, after "the fall", where God inquires of how the ultimate sin occurred and Adam's response is "*The woman whom <u>thou gavest to be with me</u>, she gave me of the tree, and I did eat*" It is the influence upon the man that makes visible the intention God had for the woman when he created her.

Adam's response tells us that Eve's position next to him was an assignment by God. He placed her by his side. God created her to *impact the environment which she shared with man*. However, the impact of woman was intended to be purposeful and godly. This can only happen if she *remains* in her true God-given identity. This requires her to stay fastened in the presence of God through *a dynamic divine partnership*.

The influence of Eve was costly. God intended for her to be a helper, to help *keep* the order of the garden and the command of God. This was the purpose of the innate influence she carried; it was for her to be a *keeper*- to sustain according to God's will.

Woman was not merely created for the increase of the human race; but was intended to operate in accountability to protect and preserve the will of God as it relates to the human race and the advancement of the Kingdom of God among them. She is entrusted with the vision of God over the space she is *"put"*.

Therefore, she is deployed for service into a space on earth to ensure that God's will prevails in that space. Usually, we find that women are being called to enlarge and expand the "seed of men" that exists in the place where she is "put". However, she can only do this successfully if she executes in partnership with God.

Unfortunately, Eve's influence was impaired by the craftiness of the serpent, and this led her to lure Adam to the ultimate sin which led to the greatest fall of mankind. It is critical to note that the change in Adam and Eve did not happen until Adam took the bite. Which means that it was the actions of the man that is binding.

This is why it was so important for him not to be alone but with a suitable helper, a keeper to help guard his mind and actions so that the word and will of God could be honored.

Genesis 3:6-7 states "And <u>when the woman saw</u> that the tree was good for food, and that it was pleasant to the eyes, and a tree to be desired to make one wise, she took of the fruit thereof, and did eat, and gave also unto her husband with her; and <u>he did eat. And the eyes of them both were opened, and they knew that they were naked;</u> and they sewed fig leaves together, and made themselves aprons."

Your vision as a woman is entirely important as it impacts the protection, prosperity, and productivity of the people in the environment in which you are connected. Eve allowed the serpent to dictate what she *"saw"*. He distorted her vision. Your vision directly impacts your influence.

The execution of your influence as woman brings forth a binding action that issues a fate for generations to come. You are powerful through your impact and influence which is necessary to help you keep your space in submission to the will of God; this is your fruitfulness.

Well aware of the level of power He had afforded Eve, God in Genesis 3:13 inquires of her *"What is this that thou hast done?"* This indicates that there was a sense of betrayal. The very creation of God meant to seal his design of man seemed to have corrupted it. It appeared to be a glitch, woman operated in a way contrary to her design because of her influence, the powerful uniqueness of her, was tainted by the serpent's deceit upon her vision.

The very nature of the woman's biological design with her having a womb to bring forth life from the seed of man is astonishing. She pulls out of him seed, incubates that seed, and brings forth life from that man. Hence, her influence and dominance is attached to the "seed" she receives from a man; the *access* he allows her for shared rulership.

It affords you the opportunity to operate and create under the authority he shares. The challenge for the woman is to expand it, to *carry* it to a length and depth that is aligned with God's design for it. This can only be done successfully through a dynamic divine partnership with God.

A woman's influence is therefore contingent upon the access that she has been granted by man; the authority he extends to her whether through his seed or otherwise. She operates from his "platform of authority". Once she has access she has freedom to influence; to use her access for the advancement of the kingdom of God.

She is capable of the same spiritually. She incubates the visions of heaven through her influence. This incubating that she does involves *"sowing seeds"* in her space of dominance. These seeds make take the form of prayers, words, or deeds, which when rooted, blossom into their fullness at a time determined by God.

So, woman by all aspects of understanding given the magnitude of her influence is expected to enhance and increase the environment for which she is attached in *partnership with God.*

The only way she can successfully do this is by guarding and keeping the space, keeping the ground fertile for the production of divine fruit. Just as the womb presents itself as a healthy environment for the growth of the baby, the influence of a woman in any space is the incubator for heaven's plans and promises. *She is a keeper. She is a sustainer.*

I resolve that just as the earth needs the womb of the woman to sustain its population, Heaven needs the influence of a woman to birth its visions into the earth for the advancement of the

Kingdom of God. Women are critically necessary to earthly and heavenly progression.

As a woman, you have ultimate impact. If you are to rule effectively by your influence, you need to be partnered with God through the Holy Spirit. You need a well-developed line of constant communication, where you can receive leadership on exactly how to deploy your influences to see the plans of God manifested in the sphere which you have been placed.

Steadfast prayer is a woman's first line of defense in this regard. A woman cannot keep or give birth to the will of God unless she leads a lifestyle of fervent, earnest, and consistent prayer. It is her influence, *purified by prayer*, that acts as the womb for kingdom business to be accomplished on earth. We see this very clearly with the story of Queen Esther (as recorded in the Old Testament Book of *Esther*).

Esther was placed in the King's Palace by divine favor ultimately to be used to save her people which would come from her influence on the King's actions as his wife. What is most notable here is that Esther, challenged to execute her influence to save her people from death, sought the direction of the Lord and called her people to join in with her for fast and prayer before any actions were taken by her. She ensured that she was operating with a healthy influence.

There is a big difference in how the scenes played out for both Esther and Eve. However, we know that they were both women with the innate ability to rule by their natural influence.

Their rulership hinged highly upon how they protected their influence by keeping their vision pure and untarnished. The only way to keep the purity of this influence that we still carry today, as women, is to stay connected in prayer under the divine leadership of our heavenly Father. This affords a dynamic divine partnership that will bring forth your divine fruit in your sphere of influence.

You are woman, you are powerful by your influence, you were made to persist, and you were made to protect the plans of heaven on earth. Keep your vision pure and untarnished through constant communication with God. You are a valuable partner to Heaven.

Use your influence purposely- under the direction of God through the Holy Spirit. Then and only then will we see heaven moving on earth powerfully. You are the crowning glory of all creation; show up in this authority and birth your divine fruit through pure and godly influence.

Chapter 5

I Know Who I Am!

We've talked about the various dimensions of who we are, now it is time to affirm these truths. It is imperative that there is a confident understanding of who you are as you traverse the difficult seasons of your life and *birth your divine fruit*.

When you have identity, not just any identity, but your identity in Christ which is built on a certainty that nothing can break you, it may shake but it will not destroy you. The strength and power of you as God's own daughter, a woman made in his image and likeness, is the beauty of you! You carry the innate design to conquer and overcome- just like your Father!

Knowing who you are is critical in being able to push powerfully through your deepest despair to birth the visions of heaven attached to your name. Daughter, you are woman. Created intentionally and solely for fruitfulness. God expects you to show up in your divine design; birthing divine fruit in your sphere of influence.

You do not need to look for value, worth and validation externally to affirm who you are. You've been validated and certified from the time you were conceived in your mother's womb. The world and anything of it has no authority to define you because it doesn't know you. If you are a child of faith, you have the belief that you are in the world and not of the world. You have a shiftless understanding that you are completely of God; every fiber of you!

There is a pressing call on you show up in the physical world as you are represented in the spiritual world. Know that you are more than the roles and titles that the world ascribes to you. Heaven has called you into rulership and given you powerful influence over your specific domain as a woman.

You now have the knowledge you need to represent your father well. Daughter, you have the authority to bring forth new life in this world. You have the God-given authority to be *fruitful and multiply*. Honor the beauty of your design. Be relentless in showing up in your authority so that you can push powerfully, and emerge from all of life's valleys phenomenally, and fruitfully. Let's affirm this with authority. I want you to connect deeply within yourself. Take your hand and hold your heart to center your mind and speak these words powerfully from your spirit so that your soul takes note:

"I know who I am. I am a child of God created in his image and likeness and given authority to rule in the earth. I have divine authority. I am made to effectively influence my space, giving birth to the plan and purposes of heaven through my divine fruit.

The world and its worries do not define me. I carry a heavenly presence within me here on earth. This is my strength. I am an eternal being having life and impact that extends beyond the borders of this world. I am a creation of God made in his likeness, I am the daughter of the most sovereign King...I am woman!"

Powerful Actions and Reflections

POWERFUL ACTION

Write a *personal declaration* based on your divine creation in the image and likeness of God. Ensure that this declaration is based on scripture. Personalize the scripture so that it resonates completely with you.

Repeat it at least three times a day. Your whole being needs to take note of who you truly are as God's and His daughter - and certainly who you are as WOMAN- Heaven-sent helper on the earth.

Write a *powerful prayer*. Present a scripture that testifies to the great power of a woman. Also, choose a fruitful woman from the scriptures whose works you admire.

Ask God to help the essence of the scripture and characteristics of the woman to arise in you. Ask the Holy Spirit to increase your wisdom so you may execute your influence in a godly manner for the advancement of the Kingdom of God.

POWERFUL REFLECTION

PUSH Principle 1: POWERFUL PERSON

How has this PUSH principle fortified your mindset for divine birthing?

What truths about yourself, your influence and your divine fruit were introduced to you here?

How will you use this principle to step into a divine partnership with God?

Has the principle made you more confident about your ability to fight through difficulties and emerge fruitfully?

What reservations do you have?

WRITE YOUR THOUGHTS AND TAKEAWAYS HERE

YOUR PUSH POWER

 You Were Made in the **IMAGE** and **LIKENESS** of God;

 You Were Created to **RULE**;

 You Have **INFLUENCE** as a Woman to Birth the Plans of Heaven in the World Through **PARTNERSHIP WITH GOD**;

 You Need **NO VALIDATION** of Your Identity From the World;

 You Must Create **INTIMACY** with The Father, God, to Access Your Innate Power and Authority.

PUSH PRINCIPLE
TWO

POWERFUL
Purpose

Chapter 6

Anointed and Appointed

When you know the truth of your identity you come to realize that there is true purpose attached to your life. You come to know that there are people that need your anointing to not only survive but thrive. With these people in mind and heart, you fight to push powerfully through life's disruptions to serve them your *divine fruit*.

It is no coincidence and no mistake that you are in the world today. Your presence in the world is an appointment with heaven. You have been handpicked, purposefully made, and selected to carry out an assignment here on earth. This appointment was written in the books from the time of your conception. Jeremiah 1:5 states: *"Before I formed thee in the belly I knew thee; and before thou camest forth out of the womb I sanctified thee, and I ordained thee a prophet unto the nations."*

Your life is bigger than you. You are here to serve. You are a timely solution for a people, a deliverer! There are people right around you waiting to be served by you; to be freed and enriched. You are obligated to show up with your *divine fruit* as your reasonable service! People's lives depend on you - *yes you!* Your life is a journey to your fruitful form; your place of impact. Like any other journey there will be highs and lows. The challenge is to push through the low points to serve the people set apart just for you!

This journey is special. There are more than 8 billion people in the world and no two people will have the same experience of life- no two will birth the same divine fruit. Just as you are unique your fruit is peculiar as well. There is no substitute for it. This is the beauty of your life and your influence; it is special and very personal.

You are the right woman for the job! Say this with me *"I am the one! I was born just for it!"* The key is receiving vision and understanding about the assignment. Again, this requires intimacy with the one that has anointed and appointed you for the assignment. Jeremiah 29:11 states "For I know the thoughts that I think toward you, saith the Lord, thoughts of peace, and not of evil, to give you an expected end.

You, my dear sister, are a faithful steward for the Lord. That means there must be a realization that you are being led by the *Good Shepherd,* and this should present itself as a privilege and honor to you because He leads in the paths of righteousness- for His name's sake. So, wherever He leads you, He must act in a way that will preserve the integrity of His name. Hence, being in a dynamic divine partnership with God is safe and worthwhile.

There is a way that we fulfill our assignment to birth your divine fruit and that is through Jesus Christ by the Holy Spirit. John 15:5 states *"I am the vine, ye are the branches: He that abideth in me, and I in him, the same bringeth forth much fruit: for without me ye can do nothing."*

<u>Fruitfulness is partnership with God.</u> **God is looking for a willing and committed partner in you.** He wants you to work closely with him to bear the *divine fruit* of your assignment. Partnership with the Lord is a call that will stretch you. He often calls you to something that is completely out of your league and

comfort because He wants you to arise in faith; He wants your complete reliance on Him. The assignment will always seem far bigger than you, and that is because it will require you to step into a more heightened awareness of yourself; a more authentic you. A place you can only access by faith- the place of your *divine fruit*.

God called Moses and Jeremiah to speak and both said to Him they could not, the assignment and call seemed beyond them. God has called me to write this book and I too considered this beyond me. I did not appear to be the best in Literary Arts; I vividly remember scoring a D in my high school Language finals. This failure sealed the deal for me to push forward with a career in accounting. Writing, I thought, was not my best skillset. Years later, still remembering the sting of that D grade, I counted myself out immediately upon the call. However, God made this appointment unequivocally clear to me, and it never left my heart.

This book was presented to me in a vision in 2017; Heaven literally called my name profoundly three times, and when I refused to answer there came into my mind's eye a book. *I knew the assignment.* What I didn't know, however, was that the assignment was not based on my ability, but my availability. God was just waiting for my *"Yes!"* to a *dynamic divine* partnership with Him. He was waiting for a demonstration of faith from me which presented itself as a willing, open, and surrendered heart ready for the call.

This is the beauty of the *dynamic divine partnership*. This is how you know that the work you are called to do is not of you. You are stepping into spaces would normally be uncomfortable for you, and you are occupying and operating in them with a delegated authority. I am literally writing right now and waiting on the next powerful words to be uttered through the Holy Spirit; the epitome of divine partnership. I am yet only a vessel for the work of God to flow from Heaven into the earth so that God's people prosper.

When God has appointed you, you will never have to do it alone. There is a well-known quote that states, *"God doesn't call the qualified, he qualifies the called."* All He really needs is your absolute yes and He will bridge every single gap in the process.

Do not be afraid. You simply need a heart posture that is open to receive direction from Him. He needs your *full surrender*. He needs your *complete obedience*. He needs you to be dedicated to seeing his work and plans materialize in the earth. This is never easy; it is always usually a fight. But, He needs you to be audacious about birthing your *divine fruit-* your people need it; the Kingdom of God does not advance on earth without it.

This call to *divine birthing* is a call to be about your Father's business.

Time is of the essence; be swift to answer the call!

Chapter 7
Many Are The Plans

Proverbs 19:21 states *"There are many devices in a man's heart; nevertheless the counsel of the Lord, that shall stand."* Many times, we want to grab the bull by the horns and run full speed ahead with our own plans. As humans, we were made very intelligent and creative individuals, so there is no limit to the permutations and combinations of plans that we make and follow to fulfill our own hearts desires.

Because God allows us free will in leading our lives, He will allow us to plan for a lifetime. However, we find that most often those plans are not of God, and they almost always lead us to a reckoning. With our limited views, we plan without the understanding of the full story at play.

Most of the time our plans are fully centered around us and our desires at that moment with a little splash of God, because somehow, we recognize we need will need him to breathe on it to give it life.

So, here it is, we present this colorful and sometimes very scheduled plan to God, and we petition for His favor towards us so heaven can manifest it, and not once do we inquire of Him if our plan is according to His will.

We just know that the scripture of Matthew 7:7 says, *"Ask, and it shall be given you; seek, and ye shall find; knock, and it shall be opened unto you."* We fail to submit our agendas to God. We don't want to get on board with God's plans. Instead, we want God to jump on our train and that is completely out of order!

Prayer is a petition. We go before God with our requests and plans and we ask Him to see them through. However, when our plans are not aligned with His we cannot expect our petition to be answered in our favor.

How can we present plans through prayer that will receive the endorsement of Heaven and ultimately be manifested on earth? In order to receive a blessing and see our petitions fulfilled, they have to be aligned with the agenda of God; they must serve the purposes of God. Prayers that serve the purposes of Heaven get the attention of God. Those are the prayers that receive answers.

Consider the story of Hannah (as recorded in 1 Samuel chapters 1 and 2), her greatest desire was for a child. She was barren and pleaded and petitioned to God to show favor and to open her womb so she might bear a child. In her praying to God, she submitted to Him that if He were to grace her with this child she would dedicate his life back to God, she would give him up for service in the temple of the Lord.

Hannah understood the power of an effective prayer. She understood that her desire must somehow collide with the purposes of God and His kingdom. They couldn't be mutually exclusive, they had to exist in each other. They were mutually beneficial.

Are your plans serving God in a significant way? When you present them in prayer, can they attract His attention and all the blessings that come along with it? *"How will this serve God?"* should be the first question you ask of your desires. You must be confident in the ability of those desires to serve the Kingdom of God; to prosper the people of God.

You must be able to envision it working on God's behalf and not just selfishly for you. How will God get the glory out of this? Can you see the glory of God arising from this desire? Is it truly purposeful to God? *Is it fruitful?*

When we submit our lives to the purposes of God, we can be assured that the pain and troubles will make sense at the end of the day. One thing about life is we will run into problems that will bring us pain, this is definite. John 16:33 assures us *"In the world ye shall have tribulation: but be of good cheer; I have overcome the world."*

The pains and difficulties of life can become very distracting and attempt to disarm us of our God-given authority. It may dare to force us into a space of surrender. However, it is meant to align us, to move us into the perfect position to seek the will of God.

You must not discredit the pain; it is more than a bad feeling. While you are charged with the huge responsibility to endure it; it is also working to direct and lead you. Let it do its work.

Don't be too quick to just pray it away. Carry the pain before the throne of God and inquire about the message the pain bears; what the pain is trying to say to you? One thing is for sure, there is a hidden message for you within.

In God's plan, the pain will be constructive. We are more inclined to endure the pain with good posture when we know that it points to a worthy end. We cannot promise the same from our own plans. This is the beauty of submitting to God's plan.

We will stay fastened in place and hold on, when we know without a shadow of a doubt that the glory of God must arise from the ashes of the difficulties; it has to! *The Lord's good purpose will prevail!*

God can also use our failed plans and setbacks to beckon us toward Him if we decide to submit to Him. When we quit trying to lead our own lives and acknowledge the sovereign lordship of God, we make all the failures of our past selfish plans worth it.

Romans 8:28 states *"And we know that all things work together for good to them that love God, to them who are the called according to his purpose."* Those failures now become critical and constructive components of the beautiful plan of God. They no longer stand in isolation, but they are the qualifying factors; the stepping stones and the leverage to a *phenomenally fruitful* version of you as revealed through the plan of God.

It's much like going to a car dealership and requesting a trade-in. You will now be able to take your old plans and failures, *as is*, and trade them in for a plan that is bigger and better than you could ever imagine, *the plan of God*. This plan of God assures you the best possible life. One of prosperity, abundance, and fruitful impact.

Jesus states in John 10:10 *"I am come that they might have life, and that they might have it more abundantly"* The only way to this abundant life which extends into eternal life is through the plan of God. There is a rebirth under the plan of God; a *"newness"*.

The scriptures of 2 Corinthians 5:17 affirms, *"Therefore if any man be in Christ, he is a new creature: old things are passed away; behold, all things are become new."* This is an outstanding offer to us, and it should not be ignored or refused. There is no one that can strategize and plan like the sovereign Lord.

I will continually testify to it all the days of my life. The way that I have seen God order the steps of my life when I surrendered it all to Him leads me to think of Him as *Master Orchestrator*. There is no one that can do it better than He can.

The plan of God gives you full coverage. You are completely protected under it. You won't have to be concerned about losses and shortfalls because they are all very well taken care of by God.

Rest confidently and contently in His plan.

His plan —as rigid as it may seem sometimes is a place of peace and prosperity because you know without reservation that it all culminates in fruitfulness - this is a guarantee under God's plans.

Chapter 8
Where Is My Rome?

You must know exactly where God wants you to go. There are details of your assignment that God will reveal to you once you become intimately connected with Him through a dynamic divine partnership.

"*Rome*" represents just this. It represents the destination where God is leading you to complete the assignment; the vision of the fullness of your fruitfulness. There will be other assignments, and points of service, that must be completed before you arrive to the place of culmination- *the ultimate place of impact*. You need a destination that will keep you anchored in the disruptions and chaos of life. One that will evoke a willpower to stay steadfast and push through the valleys because there are a particular people, at a particular place(s), waiting for you to show up and serve them with your particular fruit.

This concept of Rome is based on the apostle Paul's journey specifically documented in the New Testament book of Acts. Paul was a great apostle who came after the resurrection and ascension of Jesus. He was a church planter responsible for spreading the gospel of Christ to the Jews and the Gentiles. He was completely committed to his assignment. However, Paul was not always on this side of the gospel. He was born Saul and was a Jew – a

Pharisee who worked assiduously to persecute believers of the day.

The interesting thing about this is, he considered his work in persecution a sincere defense of the Jewish faith. The scripture records that, as he was on his way to Damascus to persecute the church there, he had an experience with God that left him blind but opened the eyes of his heart to the truth of the Christian movement and message. As a result, Saul was converted, and this was evidenced by the change in his name to Paul.

During that experience with God, Paul humbled himself before God and inquired as to the work that God had set apart for him. He inquires of God in Acts 22:10 *"What shall I do, Lord?"*. This is where God gave him an understanding of the charge on his life; how he was expected to carry the good news of the gospel to the Jews and the Gentiles alike.

Ironically, Paul himself who was a master persecutor faced a lot of persecution in executing his assignment. Most of which came from the Jews, his very own people. He was beaten, imprisoned, constantly threatened, shipwrecked, and even bitten by a snake while on this journey. Further, there were Jews that fasted, and refused to eat until their attempts to capture and kill him were successful.

In Acts 20: 23-24 Paul states *"the Holy Ghost witnesseth in every city, saying that bonds and afflictions abide me. But none of these things move me, neither count I my life dear unto myself, so that I might finish my course with joy, and the ministry, which I have received of the Lord Jesus, to testify the gospel of the grace of God."*

There were perhaps times in ministry when Paul got discouraged as everything came up against him, but God constantly encouraged him and reassured him that heaven was supporting him.

While being caught in a shipwreck, the angel of God assured him that no life would be lost. This served to strengthen Paul for his journey. In another incident, Paul was exasperated by the stubbornness of the Jews as recorded in Acts 18:5-6 *"Paul was pressed in the spirit and testified to the Jews that Jesus was Christ. And when they opposed themselves, and blasphemed, he shook his raiment, and said unto them, your blood be on your own heads; I am clean; from henceforth I will go unto the Gentiles"*

Then God, who in His sovereign authority, had commissioned Paul for this work encouraged him for the race; *strengthened* him for the assignment. According to Acts 18:9-11: *"Then spake the Lord to Paul in the night by a vision, Be not afraid, but speak, and hold not thy peace: For I am with thee, and no man shall set on thee to hurt thee: for I have much people in this city. And he continued there a year and six months, teaching the word of God among them."*

One thing that God did make clear to Paul was that no matter how things around him seemed to be unraveling that he would make it to Rome, which was where his teaching and preaching of the gospel would end. Acts 23:11 states: *"And the night following the Lord stood by him, and said, Be of good cheer, Paul: for as thou hast testified of me in Jerusalem, so must thou bear witness also at Rome."*

This gave Paul the confidence he needed to finish the race strong. He knew that God would protect, provide, and show him favor as he led him through his journey to his final destination of Rome. Paul had a definite destination, and he was determined to get there because he knew it was the will of Heaven. It was what

Heaven required of his life. In Acts 26:19, Paul states *"I was not disobedient unto the heavenly vision."*

You, like Paul, have a Rome! Ask God to show you what you should be heading towards, where He is leading you, where He is carrying you, and where your journey culminates. He will answer! Refuse to move until you hear from God. His word promises that He responds when you seek him wholeheartedly.

Knowing your purposed destination builds within you a stamina and determination to push through. You will develop a dedication and discipline that cannot be easily quenched because you know with a certainty what God has willed for you. It begs you to push relentlessly through the chaos to see divine fruit emerge from your life according to God's plan for you.

This seeking requires a lot of *prayer and fasting*. Intimate time pressing into the presence of God so that He can unfold the mystery of Heaven involving you to you. God honors sincerity and purity of heart. He gives attention to a diligent seeker. Go before Him hungry, humbled, and willing. Sit relentless with Him, seek, and ask until your heart receives the answer.

In John 4:34 after being urged to eat by his disciples Jesus responds, *"My meat is to do the will of him that sent me, and to finish his work."* What is your food today? What is fueling you to continue? Are you powered by the will and the work of God? Are you driven by a great desire to birth your divine fruit?

I came to a point in my life where I refused to believe that life was simply a never-ending cycle of pain and chaos. Someway, somehow, it had to make sense and God would be the only one to show me how. I surrendered and humbled myself before the Lord. I sought Him relentlessly for my *Rome*. After knocking on the doors of heaven ceaselessly and desperately by prayer, He answered.

When the vision for my life was revealed to me, I was left in complete awe, almost perplexed. I was on my bathroom floor in prayer when He showed me the vision of global impact on women, across specific places. *Me? How could I?* I am broken and disenfranchised. His response was simple but powerful "*I will show you.*" Which meant I would have to follow His leading. Again, an invitation to a *dynamic divine partnership* with Him.

There was no way I could share this with anyone who knew me, they would surely believe my mental state was compromised. Much like Joseph when he shared his dream with his brothers in which they were all kneeling to him. Even his father, who loved him dearly, questioned its authenticity and rebuked him (Genesis 37).

God's plans for you are massive! They are *exceedingly greater and more abundant* than you could ever imagine! You are powerful with the understanding of the work God has assigned to you. When you understand the assignment, you'll have tunnel vision as your heart becomes completely *submitted to service;* the birth of your divine fruit.

You know now where God needs you to be, and you know without a doubt, that your work is not done until you reach to each point revealed to you. There is no stopping until the work is done.

It doesn't matter the weather: rain, hail, or storm, you are pushing through because there is a job to be done and people are waiting for you- they are waiting for your *divine fruit*! You must make it there! *Know your Rome!* It is your vision, and this vision is indeed essential. The scripture in Proverbs 29:18 urges us, "*where there is no vision, the people perish"*. Paul had the full vision of heaven concerning his life, and this is why he remained fruitful and impactful throughout his time.

His eyes stayed on the vision, and he refused to give up until he saw it come to fruition on earth. Paul bore a fruit that last. Thousands of years later and we are still inspired by his work in this present day.

Do you have the vision of heaven concerning your life?

Do you have a picture of the fullness of your *divine fruit*?

Do you know where your service will culminate?

Tell me, where *is your Rome?*

Chapter 9
Be Fruitful and Multiply

Fruitfulness is truly not an option. It is a command of us from the time of creation. Genesis 1:28 states: *"And God blessed them, and God said unto them, Be fruitful, and multiply, and replenish the earth and subdue it."* Fruitfulness is faithfulness; it indicates that you honor the creation of God in you and you desire to see him glorified through His very creation- you!

The story of the fig tree as presented in *Mark 11*, clearly presents the importance of fruitfulness to Jesus. Here we see a famished Jesus approaching what looks like a flourishing and abundant fig tree from a distance, only to be utterly disappointed when He reaches the tree and finds no fruit.

Jesus, in response to this unfruitfulness, cursed the tree and it withered and died. This signifies that purpose is important to God, and failing to live and produce according to purpose, prevents the manifestation of the glory of God into the earth.

Jesus understood the principles of Heaven. He understood that Heaven expected creation to do what it was designed to do. He also understood that anything not acting in alignment with this design went against the will of Heaven and really had no right to exist and take up space on earth just to "look the part". The tree had the correct appearance, but the tree held no fruit. It failed to contribute to earth as it was commanded to by its design.

Don't let this be you! Be fruitful as you are commanded. A fruitful tree stands confidently! It has no question as to why it is here because it does what it is supposed to do in its season. It is committed to bearing because it knows that there are a famished people depending on it, awaiting its fruit to be fed.

Knowing what God has called you to do is a critical part of becoming fruitful. Not only must you know, but you must also operate in it. You are called to this service and your life must be centered around it because it is why you were created. You were deployed here to earth for a particular task and to be used for anything other than that task is to be unfruitful.

God is glorified when you show up and produce in a manner consistent with your divine design- this gives credence to Him as a creator. When people around you experience the good and fruitful works that pour out of you; they will attribute all glory to God and be drawn to praise His name (Matthew 5:16). This is the ultimate goal of your existence and the epitome of fruitfulness- the manifestation of the good glory of God.

Fruitfulness requires sacrifice as it often requires you to deny your personal desires to follow the call of God. Fruitfulness brings you to the understanding that your life is not about you, but it serves a greater good; it is so much bigger than you!

Think about it, a tree does not bear fruit to serve itself; it cannot use the fruit that it bears. This is so because its purpose is to serve outside of itself. The same holds true for you! Alongside your *divine fruit* is a people that need it to thrive.

Your refusal to align yourself with your heavenly design deprives them of what is needed for their own purpose and prosperity. Your life is interconnected with so many others in the world. You are not to take your contribution for granted because you are a critical part of the massive plan of the Kingdom of God; you do not exist in isolation. Hence, you have an obligation to act responsibly when it comes to birthing your *divine fruit*.

Your fruitfulness gives others permission to act in fruitfulness as well. Those that eat of your fruit will be inspired to blossom and bloom into a productive form thereby impacting lives with the *divine fruit* you have helped to bear in them.

Real fruit multiplies, it doesn't stop at you. It does not benefit you because it is really not to "feed" you. It bears seeds which when planted produce an abundance of its kind. It is fruit that lasts.

John 15:16 states *"Ye have not chosen me, but I have chosen you, and ordained you, that ye should go and bring forth fruit, and that your fruit should remain."* Get excited about your *divine fruit* and the faith-filled generations that will spring forth from it.

Your fruitfulness goes beyond the form of your actual physical works but also shows up in the person that you are. It is about the elevation of your character. It is a demonstration of your transformation as you become more like Christ. As you bear your *divine fruit*, you should see more of the *Fruits of the Spirit* manifesting in your daily living and relation to others.

This is a profound change that truly affords us a heavenly experience on earth. Galatians 5: 22-23 states, *"But the fruit of the Spirit is love, joy, peace, longsuffering, gentleness, goodness, faith, meekness, temperance: against such things there is no law."*

Birthing the divine fruit of your womb begets a *change in you*. It requires you to evolve from season to season. This transformation is due to the increase of the Holy Spirit within you and makes you fit for a great harvest.

How has your harvest been lately?

Has it been bountiful?

Chapter 10
I Know The Call On My Life!

A person who has a God-given fruitful destination is unbreakable and powerful! You know what Heaven requires of you and you are fully confident that Heaven will provide for what it has purposed. You are completely covered because you now stand in the purpose of God and only His purpose prevails. It has to, if only for His name's sake.

You are doing what you were designed to do and that validates your place here on earth; it necessitates your existence. You don't need anything in this world to affirm or validate the fact that you are needed here because Heaven already did! Heaven approved you from before the time you were formed in your mother's womb! *You belong here*. Fight like it. Live in your authority!

I call on you to inquire of God about your design and destination! Ask him to give you a picture of your fruitfulness. *"Where is my Rome, Lord?"* should be your continuous cry. He will open his plan up to you beautifully as he shows you what you were called to do, and who you were called to influence with your *divine fruit*. He will reveal the fullness of your fruitfulness.

The chaos of life does not define you. They are only occurrences, leave them as such, don't give them the power to name you. The world cannot render you a fate, that would be highly presumptuous of it because it simply does not know you. Only heaven knows and understands the depth of your fruitfulness; who you are, what you have been created and purposed to do, and who you were meant to serve.

Affirm the power of your purpose and fruitfulness with me:

"I am fearfully and wonderfully created, set-apart, anointed, and appointed from the time I was conceived for a special work and for a special people.

It is my kingdom duty to birth the divine fruit that God has designed just for me; I put aside my desires and fears and go wholeheartedly after the will of God.

I will powerfully impact my people. Those that eat of my fruit will be inspired by faith to bring forth fruits of their own kind.

I humbly and willing pledge my faithfulness to God's vision and design over my life.

I live and breathe for the purposes of God.

Greater works will spring out of me and prevail in the earth for the glory of God!"

Powerful Actions and Reflections

POWERFUL ACTION

Get your journal and write for ten minutes non-stop about what God has appointed and anointed you to do. Don't worry about well-constructed sentences- allow them to flow out of your heart onto the paper freely. Ask the Holy Spirit to guide you into all truth before you begin writing.

Write a *powerful prayer*. Ask God to clearly show you your Rome. Ask the question that Paul asked in his conversion encounter with God, "What shall I do Lord?"

Write a *vision statement and a mission statement* based on this revelation. Submit your vision and mission statement to Him. Ask God to purify it, ask him to show you where it needs to be more aligned with the will of Heaven, if necessary. Watch and listen expectantly for his response and adjust your vision and mission appropriately. Once you are confident about God's word concerning your vision and mission post it in a place where you can clearly see and read it every day.

POWERFUL REFLECTION

PUSH Principle 2: POWERFUL PURPOSE

How has this PUSH principle fortified your mindset for divine birthing?

What truths about yourself, your influence, and your divine fruit were introduced to you here?

How will you use this principle to step into a divine partnership with God?

Has the principle made you more confident about your ability to fight through difficulties and emerge fruitfully?

What reservations do you have?

WRITE YOUR THOUGHTS AND TAKEAWAYS HERE

YOUR PUSH POWER

 You were created and commanded to be **FRUITFUL**.

 You have a specific **PURPOSE** & **PEOPLE**; you are special.

 Your fruit has the ability to multiply and be impactful on the earth; this is your **SERVICE**.

 You don't have to figure it all out on your own. Once you submit, God will guide you into how to access and occupy the realm of your **POWER**.

PUSH PRINCIPLE
THREE

POWERFUL
Presence

Chapter 11
The Word Is Life

You were not created to do life alone. You were given the great gift of the presence of God through His Holy Spirit, the great advocate, to help you push powerfully through the chaotic scenes of life to your *fruitfulness*.

The Holy Spirit is increased in you as you dwell in the word of God, commit to prayer, live a life of praise, and continually declare the promises of God over your life. The word of God is your foundation. It is the solid base that you use to build a relationship and partnership with God through Jesus Christ His Son. The word of God is core to your fruitful mindset; your level of prayer and praise is derived from the density of the Word that is rooted and dwelling within you.

It's simply more than just knowing scripture, but it is your meditation on the Word that allows it to penetrate your spirit and become a part of who you are. This union with the Word creates in you an unquenchable urge to push compelling your *divine fruit* to come forth.

It is the word that transforms you so that you can take hold of who God is and who you are as a child of God. It fosters a mindset of faith and fruitfulness that allows you to stand confidently in your assignment.

The scripture of John 6:63 states *"It is the spirit that quickeneth; the flesh profiteth nothing; the words that I speak unto you, they are spirit, and they are life."* Hence, who you are today in Christ and how you stand, is deeply dependent on the propensity of the Word within you.

Allow the Word to dwell so deep that you become impregnated with the Spirit of God. The scriptures also remind us that the word of the Lord is imperishable, that heaven and earth will pass away, but the word of God stands forever.

There is an ultimate authority that stands in the word of God, *the living word of God*. God is one with His word; He doesn't deviate from it. The book of Hebrews 4:12 tells *"for the word of God is quick, and powerful, and sharper than any two-edged sword, piercing even to the dividing asunder of soul and spirit, and of the joints and marrow, and is a discerner of the thoughts and intents of the heart"* this is powerful!

Receiving the word of God and meditating on it day and night is building the Spirit within you. You may also meditate on the word by sharing it with those around you. Inviting others to embrace the power of the word.

This increases the Spirit within you; it magnifies the presence of God with you. It is the recognition and acknowledgment of God's constantly abiding presence that is the abundant source of your strength and courage.

As the Spirit grows within you by way of the Word, it transforms your mind thereby renewing your thinking and living. Yes, the word is a thought system by which you live and eventually embody. The word is the basis of your faith in God and His son Jesus Christ and, Hebrews 11:6 explains to us it is *impossible to please God without faith*. You cannot be *fruitful* without faith. Your *fruitfulness* is most pleasing unto God.

Psalm 1: 1-3 tells us *"Blessed is the man that walketh not in the counsel of the ungodly, nor standeth in the way of sinners, nor sitteth in the seat of the scornful.* ***But his delight is in the law of the Lord; and in his law doth he meditates day and night. And he shall be like a tree planted by the rivers of water, That bringeth forth his fruit in his season; His leaf also shall not wither; And whatsoever he doeth shall prosper.*** *"*

This is evidence of the abundance of life that is encompassed in the word of God; the *living* word of God.

The Word is your primary defense. How you choose to dwell within it determines the strength of your foundation. Everything flows from your level of intimacy with the Word. Your confidence in the presence of God who is with you through your toughest times is a direct factor of how you feast on the Word daily.

Jesus himself asserted in Matthew 4:4 that *"man shall not live by bread alone, but by every word that proceedeth out of the mouth of God."* It is the word that enlarges the powerful presence of God to strengthen and embolden you to push through every contraction of life and *birth your divine fruit.*

I sat in a Sunday morning church service and during the sermon, we were urged to sit quietly and connect with the Spirit and listen for what God was requiring of us in that very moment. This was done collectively as a church, but it was an individual search for the rhema word God wanted to release to us through our spirits.

As I sat in my pew and reverently acknowledged the presence of the Holy Spirit, I opened my spirit to receive the word of Heaven for me. One word came to me, and it was *"fasten."* It was a word that I was familiar with, I had heard it and used it multiple times.

However, I went in search for an official meaning to help bring full revelation to this word. This search revealed that the word fasten implies that an obsessive concentration is being directed toward someone or something.

God wanted me to be reminded of the need to keep my eyes on Him and the best way to do this was to dwell in the word, intensely. I needed to become more intentional in my focus, I needed to go deeper to become stronger and more confident to conquer the challenging season I was in. My intense focus on Him was required for me to *emerge fruitfully* in the place of my struggle.

It reminded me of when Jesus called out to Peter to walk on water. Peter, stricken with fear, struggled until Jesus urged him to fix his eyes on Him. Isaiah 26:3 tells us that *"thou wilt keep in perfect peace, whose mind is stayed (fastened) on thee; because he trusteth in thee."*

Being fastened is essential to being powerfully postured for the push; it builds a faith that cannot be moved. In the presence of strong faith is a peace that passes understanding; a peace that doesn't make sense given the chaotic circumstances that confront you. A peace and resolve that makes *fruitfulness* possible.

The word of God not only fortifies and deepens your understanding and awareness of God, but it simply gives you direction and wisdom on how to go about living a life that is in alignment with God. It is step-by-step guidance. It provides truth about your life and gives you access to your rights as a daughter of God.

2 Timothy 3:16-17 states, *"All scripture is given by inspiration of God, and is profitable for doctrine, for reproof, for correction, for instruction in righteousness: That the man of God may be perfect, thoroughly furnished unto all good works."* The Word is life! *Everything* you need can be found within the word of God.

In John 15:4, Jesus tells us *"abide in me, and I in you. As a branch cannot bear fruit of itself, except it abides in the vine; no more can ye, except ye abide in me".* To remain in Jesus is to remain in the living word. *God's presence is His word*, therefore, if you are looking to magnify His presence you need to largely dwell in the word. Once you do this, fruitfulness will be your portion.

This deep meditation brings you an enthusiasm about everything you encounter in the natural world. The Greek translation of enthusiasm means *"God Within"*.

As you become completely focused on the word you also become strongly fastened in your faith. Your spiritual vision has now been optimized and you begin to see differently. You began to see everything from God's view; everything now becomes beautiful and worthy.

This is an uncommon experience that only remaining buckled and rooted in the word of God will afford. It affords a new abundant perspective of your life's circumstances. It gives you access to a higher dimension that breathes a spiritual vision powerful to overcome and protect against the snares of life; simply because you think differently and therefore you see differently.

This is the freedom that Christ has died to make abundantly available to us, the freedom of the mind to be *released from the anxiety and fear* of today's trouble and remain confident in the victory that is already secured, the joy that is already set before you! The wisdom of the Word, makes it a sword in the fight to birth your divine fruit allowing you to navigate your challenges with a heightened heavenly awareness.

There is absolutely no authoritative and fruitful living in this world outside of the dwelling in the power of the living word. It is your guide and compass.

Psalm 119:105 states *"Thy word is a lamp unto my feet and a light unto my path."* It illuminates the only way you are to walk; *the way of God.*

Chapter 12

Faithful Promises

There are so many promises that God has made available to you as a *child of God through faith*. From the time of the Children of Israel who were being led out of Egypt into the Promised Land (as detailed in the Old Testament scriptures of Exodus), God has been making promises and remaining faithful to His promises. He does exactly what He says He will do because He is a God of integrity, He is one with his word. In Joshua 1:9, Joshua assumes the responsibility to lead the children of Israel into the promised land, God commands him to be strong and courageous, not to be discouraged *"for the Lord thy God is with thee <u>whithersoever thou goest</u>."* That is a promise of presence!

These promises however are largely based on our ability to stay submitted to the word and way of God. Yes, we have a choice as to whether we want to receive of his great promises. In Deuteronomy 11, God laid before the Children of Israel blessings and curses and gave them a choice. He is this same God today. He is offering you the bounty of Heaven through every promise laid out in the bible and He is desiring for you to choose to see those promises come to pass. The manifestation of these promises will require you to remain steadfast and faithful to His word. Like Abraham, your faith which is your mere belief and trust in God, considers you righteous and therefore eligible to receive of the promises of God. One of the promises I hold fast to is the promise laid forth in Hebrews 13: 5 which states that *"I will never leave thee, nor forsake thee".* This gives me the full assurance that no matter the pit I may find myself in, like Joseph who was enslaved, like Daniel who was thrown to the lions, like Job who was afflicted, and like the three Hebrew boys who were thrown into the fire- *God is with me*; *Emmanuel is right here by my side!* Psalm 23:4 testifies to this as David says, *"Yea, though I walk through the valley of the shadow of death, I will fear no evil: for thou art with me; thou rod and staff they comfort me."*

This is a major promise all throughout the scriptures as God commands those, he has appointed for kingdom assignments not to be afraid but to take courage because He is with them. The same applies to you this very day! Whether you are faced with lack or loss, despair or drawback, God wants you to know that He is in it with you! He always has been. Don't let fear hold you back! Lean on Him and PUSH to complete your earthy assignment; *fight to birth your divine fruit.*

There are also personal promises that God makes with us. He gives us visions of what He will do in our personal lives. He promised Abraham and Sarah a son and He delivered. Think about the promises God has *just for you*! These are the personal anchors for you, these are what will give a strong spirit of expectancy and cause you to push powerfully through any manner of dread because you are persuaded that there is fruit at the end. *God will make it happen.*

It was on a highway, where I came face to face with the reality of my failed and broken marriage. It was shortly after separating from my husband and I had dedicated a month for fasting to get an understanding of what God wanted of the future of our marriage. It was the twenty-second day of the month, the exact day of our marriage. It so happened that my vehicle met with my husband's vehicle randomly on a roundabout; both of us met at the same point as if we had planned it.

This was not a coincidence. God was present. It was there that the encounter happened. In his vehicle was what seemed like the perfect little family. However, the woman was not me and the child was not mine. The reality of this moment shattered the little hope I clung so desperately to.

This was all revealed by God. The encounter was seamless. I was heartbroken, for myself but even more so for my kids. I remember being so distraught that I took a walk by a canal drenched in tears. I sat on a rock by the waters, looked up to the sky, and continually asked God *"Why?"* I could not comprehend why He would allow this to happen to me and my children. The only response I continually heard from Him, which came in such a sweet reassuring voice amidst all the chaos was *"The promise is still true."*

I took a rock from the canal that day to remember the covenant with God, to remember that despite the despair that threatened to consume me, God was still bound to fulfill his promise to me of a happy, healthy, and fruitful marriage. A hope I held since childhood. I was reminded that ALL things- even the bad and the ugly- *work for the good* of those who love the Lord and are called according to His purpose (Romans 8:28). The *promises of the Father can be trusted.* They are all ready and lined up for you since your conception. They are just waiting for you to come into alignment with God, and for their appointed time. Your consistent posture of faithfulness will lead you to your promise.

Keep the promises constantly before you! Go into the scriptures and search for the promises of God that are set forth for the righteous. Go into prayer and ask God to reveal personal promises He's set aside just for you. Write these promises down. Post them on your walls. Set daily alarms in your phone to remind you of them. Make it a point to constantly keep them before you.

As Joshua 23:14 states *"And ye know in all your hearts and in all your souls, that not one thing hath failed of all the good things which the Lord your God spake concerning you; all are come to pass unto you, and not one thing hath failed thereof."* Many times, we get excited about the promises of God over our lives. We find ourselves not wanting to wait for God to direct us to it. Instead, we want to go ahead and help Him build the promise.

Please, step on the brakes! God is God! He doesn't need your help with His promise. He has already prepared the way to it for you, you will just need to *follow Him* and step into it! This simply requires acute trust as well as patience.

Your personal promises from God are your *treasury of hope.* This hope is what keeps you pushing tenaciously through the tough times to birth what Heaven wants from you- *your divine fruit.*

Cling to those promises, *they are real*, you can bank on them!

Chapter 13
Set Up Your Altar

When you stand on the word and stand on the promises of God, your praises become uncontrollable. It will flow from you like a river with no end. It will become as natural to you as breathing. Your praise is largely based on your view of God which is based on the level of intimacy you have with Him. When you know the beauty of your Father, your praise is not circumstantial. You will command your soul to bless the Lord even when it does not feel like it. The great psalmist, King David, continued to challenge his soul to rise up out of its despair and magnify the Lord. Psalm 103:2 states *"Bless the Lord, O my soul, and forget not all his benefits."*

Your soul has the tendency to be struck by and stuck in the moment. This means you have to be intentional about constantly reminding your soul of the goodness of God. *Praise is an offering.* The sweet aroma of this offering attracts the presence of God. It is inviting to Him, especially when you can set-up a praise altar in the middle of the chaos- *in the thick of your problems* and just bless Him, adorn and adore Him and thank Him for his faithfulness towards you! *Choose* to open your mouth and lift your hands in praise when your circumstances fight to make you dumb and despondent. Refuse to be bound! This is sacrifice. This is the good fruit of your lips, a worthy offering to God.

It is your praise that keeps you in a space of gratitude and contentment. In fact, all through the scriptures we are urged to act in thanksgiving and to give thanks always. This is the attitude and behavior that not only protects your heart (from which flows the issues of life), but it pours the favor of God over your life abundantly. Your praise is so important. It is your stronghold and a mighty defense in the fight to *birth your divine fruit.* God honors the praise of your lips. You can never praise God enough. *Your praise should be a lifestyle.* Your spirit should be in a state of constant praise. We've learned from the scriptures that Heaven is in constant worship. This means that God highly favors praise and worship; He holds it in high regard because it means that your attention is directed towards Him. The disruptions of life seek to entangle us emotionally so that our mouths stay closed and our hearts remain troubled. But the devil is a dirty old liar! You have got to know how to cast the distressing emotions out of your heart and mind with authority! This will allow gratefulness and glory can arise in the place where you are and you will see *your divine fruit* being ushered forth.

King David knew this best. The book of Psalms is filled with scriptures of praise, most of them in David's most troubling times. David knew how to exalt the Lord and position himself for praise no matter what was going on in his life. His adoration for God was like none other. He had a vast understanding of God's majesty, and his songs of praise clearly gave evidence to this. Your praise reveals how you see God; the magnitude of God to you. It reveals your trust and faith in him. It tells about your gratitude for the faithfulness of God, towards you. There is a level of sincerity and purity that is required for true praise.

Praise is also a humbling act. It places you in submission to the power of God. It is an outward expression suggesting that all you are and all that you have is because of the grace, mercy, and favor of God upon you. You recognize that your entire being is bound in God.

When you praise you are acknowledging the fact that there is a Lord that sustains you and you are nothing without Him. Further, your praise suggests that you have placed your trouble in His most capable hands. The jurisdiction has changed- every care and every fear you have laid it at His feet in full confidence that He will take good care of it. So, you worship Him for what you know He will do in your situation. You praise Him in advance because you have no doubt that He will do the right thing!

You know that he will get you to the fruitful place! Therefore, the outcome and results are not a concern. In your mind, *it is already done* because it is in the hands of the ruler of the Heavens and earth who sits on the throne above all. Your praise magnifies the Lord in your space and *where He is magnified, He will dwell.* Where He dwells the supernatural happens; glory arises and divine fruits come forth.

I am from the Bahamas. In 2019, we experienced Hurricane Dorian, which was historically the worst hurricane we have had to endure as an island nation. This category five hurricane took many lives. As I listened to the testimonies of survivors and their accounts of their loss, one continues to linger strongly in my heart.

A man told his story of having to leave his family in the roof of his home that was flooded at the level of the ceiling and was actively being destroyed by intense winds piece by piece. He left his home in an attempt to get his boat as a means to provide a safe refuge for his family. Once he got to the boat, he realized an important part to operate it was missing. He then found it difficult to return to his home as he was being tossed ferociously by the winds and water. He was able to grab a hold of a lamp pole and as he held on as tight as he could he recalled beginning to *praise God* for the life he was blessed with, the experiences of his life, and the provision of God in his life which has been consistent through all his years.

I really want you to get this. Don't miss the beauty of his situation. He did not ask God to save him or ask why he and his family had to endure this. He gave thanks in the midst of a category five hurricane because God deserved it no matter what!

My Great God! What a sweet aroma to heaven! This is a praise that was hard to ignore, it had to be honored by Heaven. Thankfully, the winds blew him into the safety of a balcony of a home where he found help for his family. Every time I think of this, a shout of praise pours out of me.

You better begin to praise God *right now*, right here! Wherever you are! Irrespective of what you are faced with in this moment God deserves your praise; let it flow out freely and abundantly. Lift His name far above the difficulties and problems. Remember the good deeds of God in the past and know that He is still a God with the power to deliver even now. Thank him for it, *right now*!

Daughter, give no attention to the winds of the storm that are currently tossing you to and fro. Instead, have the audacity to set up your altar mid-storm and command your soul to bless the name of your Father God, no matter how downcast it may be.

Come on, *step up your altar*!

Open your mouth, let the praises rise from the inside of you, and watch how you push through with *power to birth your divine fruit*!

Chapter 14

Pray Continually

Prayer allows you the distinct opportunity to be in constant communication with God. It allows for a *dynamic divine partnership* with Him so that you can birth your divine fruit into the earth.

Prayer is the ultimate channel of communication between Heaven and earth. It helps our spirit connect and receive from the Holy Spirit. When done with purity of heart it is the ultimate act of submission and humility. It shows your complete dependence on God. Prayer is how we make inquiry of God. It is the most powerful moment with God especially when done alone.

Your ability to push powerfully through the trials of life has a lot to do with the frequency and depth of your prayer life. Prayer, like praise, is a lifestyle. They should be considered more like twins because they go hand in hand. They are both entirely important for fruitful living.

Hebrews 11:6 tells us that God *"is a rewarder of them that diligently seek Him."* You will begin to feel and sense the presence of God with you the more you practice prayer.

Prayer is also not to be seen as a complicated and sophisticated act where you must approach God in a proficient manner with supreme eloquence. It is simply a pouring out of your heart to God in a sincere and pure manner. It is being completely broken and open before Him, entirely submitted to His order, direction, and will.

Prayer is a two-act discipline. It requires you to communicate to God in petition and supplication, but it also requires you to sit and <u>listen</u> for the word of revelation and instruction from God. It is a conversation with God, a dialogue.

This may take the form of simply sitting in silence to hear Him at the depth of your spirit or laying prostrate before him in complete reverence to receive the word He wants to reveal to you for that time. Once you are able to discern the voice of God, you are better able to follow Him into *birthing your divine fruit*.

Praying scriptures is also a good way to affirm the word of promise in your heart and mind. *Praying in tongues* is also a very empowering and strengthening experience. There are maybe times when your mind does not know how to approach prayer.

In these situations, the Spirit intercedes for you and will begin to inquire of heaven on your behalf (Romans 8:26). This is the beauty of praying in the Spirit because it knows just what you need to overcome the present pain. It is very important to be intentional about the growth of your prayer life.

Praying in tongues releases the mysteries of heaven over your life and space and calls heaven's direct attention to you. This is a gift that you can ask of the Father, and he will grant you it through His Holy Spirit.

Fasting is also a necessary discipline in the kingdom. There will be times when you will need to deny yourself of usual pleasures to focus intensely on God to hear his voice for the wisdom to overcome. Prayer is of optimal importance during such times.

Nothing of the kingdom can be accomplished without prayer. Prayer is how the greatest plans of God are accomplished. He funnels His visions and directions through prayers and guides and leads you through it by prayer. Again, prayer is the primary channel for a dynamic divine partnership with God to birth your divine fruit into the earth.

As women, it is particularly important that we understand the need and requirement of constant prayer in our lives. We are the wombs of Heaven from which divine fruits will come forth. Heaven has called us to be a *helper*, to incubate and keep the people, places and things attached to us in alignment with the will of God.

In order to do so effectively we are required to stay connected with Heaven to remain sensitive to the activity of the environments which we guard and watch to ensure the healthy birth of heavenly plans. Moreover, there is a persistence in a woman that is not present in a man that will lead her to press into heaven until a thing is properly and completely manifested on earth.

There is an *innate tenacity* of a woman that heaven is obligated to respond to. This is why Jeremiah calls for the *wailing women*, because he knew they had the *passion and persistence* to press into Heaven and draw a favorable response.

Are you pressing into heaven through prayer for your families, your communities, and your nation? You are the womb! You are the keeper and watchman for the spaces and places God has put you in.

You have the innate influence to lead everything in your sphere into alignment with the will of God. You are an intercessor by nature. This is the power of your design that will lead you to birth *your divine fruit* on earth so that the Kingdom of God is advanced.

Prayer should be a lifestyle for you; it is how you pull down the vision of heaven unto earth. It is by your prayer that people, places, and things are cultivated and *transformed* around you. It is by your prayer that God arms you with strategies to overcome treacherous seasons or simply just makes you aware of impending disruptions just a few steps away. It is my prayer that you become fruitful; *no prayer, no fruit.*

It was through prayer that God revealed to me the death of my mother. At the time, I was perplexed. My mother showed no visible signs of sickness. She was normal. I remembered coming out of that prayer confused but with the mind to encourage her to read a certain scripture. *Was God really telling me He was going to take her away?* In the following days, my mother would go moving about her daily activities just fine. I watched her intently. I said nothing to her about the word I had received through prayer. *Did I even hear God right?*

Just a few short weeks later my mom suddenly had a stroke which had her hospitalized for five months to the time of her death. I recalled that night of prayer the day of her stroke and returned to prayer about it. I remember pouring out to God listing a number of reasons why He couldn't allow my mother to be taken away from us.

And as I listened, He said *"And what else?"* as to inquire if there were any more reasons why I think she should stay. And as I presented what I thought was valid reasoning he responded,

"There is nothing on this earth that is a good enough reward for your mother."

I knew at this point that the deal was sealed. Her honor was her elevation to eternal life and only heaven could grant that. This gave me peace for a very painful time of my life. This peace came to me through prayer.

When you develop a habit of prayer your spirit is in constant communication with God and as a result, the leadership of the Holy Spirit is clearest and compelling in your life as you can discern the voice of God. You hear God clearly and He reveals to you the unknown. *What a beauty!* This is when you know you are effective in prayer.

Again, prayers should be simple and sincere. It should pour out from a contrite heart. I encourage you to pray in many forms. Pray the scriptures, write your prayers down, think them as you go about your day, say them as you are engaged in your day's work, and just keep *constantly connected* with heaven.

A big part of prayer is listening. Take time to hear God's response to you; discern his voice. You may want to write down what you hear God saying to you throughout your day as you listen intently and expectantly for His voice.

Keep the lines of communication open so that heaven knows your voice because you show up before the throne of God daily. Speak to God about everything *even the little matters* of your day, and share your life with him. He is your Father, He is your partner in Kingdom work on earth and He is also your friend.

I am constantly inspired by the prayer life that Daniel led, it was powerful and effective. He would pray and Heaven would move in response immediately! (Daniel 10:12) This is simply because *Heaven knew his voice*, he was devoted to staying connected by persistent prayer.

The scriptures tell us in James 5:16 that *"the effectual fervent prayer of a righteous man availeth much."* In John 10:27, the word also states that *"my sheep hear my voice, and I know them, and they follow me."*

The only way to have confident clarity concerning the voice of God is through a grounded discipline of listening through prayer.

It is the voice and instruction of God that will prepare you, clear the way, and give you a strategy for effective management of every trouble that confronts you as you push powerfully to conquer them all and birth your divine fruit.

Chapter 15
I Know How To Magnify The Presence of God!

Let's pause to consider Moses and his leadership of the children of Israel out of Egypt as detailed in the Old Testament scriptures of *Exodus*. This was only possible by the presence of God. The staff that Moses led with was representative of the power of God that was present with Him. I want you to know that you also are leading with a staff today filled with the power of God. Your staff is your spirit, overflowing with the Holy Spirit.

The Israelites were protected and provided for when the staff was lifted high. The Holy Spirit does the same for you when you choose to magnify Him by constantly lifting your *prayer, praise, the promises* of God, and His *precepts* high above everything else in your life. The Holy Spirit, which is the presence of God with you, will provide you with the power, protection, provision, and peace needed to birth your divine fruit. Keep your spirit high by magnifying and lifting the Holy Spirit within you.

John 14:16-17 states *"And I will pray the Father, and he shall give you another Comforter, that he may abide with you forever; even the Spirit of truth; whom the world cannot receive, because it seeth him not, neither knoweth him: but ye know him; for he dwelleth with you, and shall be in you."*

It is your call to constantly create an environment where the Holy Spirit can largely abide. To dwell in the presence of God is to open yourself up to power beyond measure. Even though we cannot see God physically, it is our complete assurance in Him that allows us to believe that He is ever-present. *You are never alone.*

When you know the word of God and have been brought to a deeper revelation of who God is and ultimately who you are, you've stepped into a dimension of true authority and power. You've now gained a confidence that cannot be shaken.

As you become familiar with the promises of God and see some of them begin to manifest in your life you gain a complete assurance of the validity of the sovereignty and integrity of God. You now have built a solid and undeniable trust in God, and, upon that trust, you push strongly past the disruptions and birth the unimaginable into the earth through your *divine fruit.*

Because you now dwell daily in the word and meditate on the promises of God, your praise and prayer *naturally flow* from your soul and spirit just as breath flows from your body. It becomes a natural expression of your union with the word and promises of God. Therefore, knowing and believing and holding fast to the word of God and the promises therein, is imperative because it determines the depth and width of your prayer and praise, and the potency of your power to push and birth your divine fruit.

Be sure to surround yourself with people who will support you in increasing in the Holy Spirit. Those that will remind you of the promises of God over your life. People like Aaron and Hur who literally held the arms of Moses up as he lifted the Staff of God high to secure victory for the Israelites- God's chosen people over the Amalekites (*Exodus 17*). People like Abigail, who rushed to deliver the great King David from the committal of a senseless act as she reminded him of the great anointing of God over his life to become king. She refused to allow him to abort those promises; she ensured that he preserved his destiny (*1 Samuel 25*).

Who is helping you raise your arm today? Who is pulling you back into alignment with the will of God and reminding you of the promises that God has over your life? Get connected with people that honor the presence of God. People who help you push powerfully and emerge fruitfully!

Allow the Holy Spirit to guard and to guide you. Open up and submit completely to Him. This is the relationship you need, for out of it flows a love that cannot be shaken; it cannot fail. When you live in the presence of God you are fit to weather the storm courageously and arise with your divine fruit.

It is His presence that makes the difference in how you show up and impact the world. 2 Timothy 1:7 states *"For God has not given us the spirit of fear; but of power, and of love, and of a sound mind."* Be bold and bountiful, get in the presence of God so you can push powerfully and emerge fruitfully!

Now let's affirm this in our lives:

"I am a woman of power and authority as delegated by the God of Heaven and the earth. I dwell in His word day and night and have been and will continue to be transformed by the power of His living word.

I have seen the promises of God in my life and will continue to step into each promise God has set aside just for me, I receive them now.

I am a woman of prayer and praise. I honor God with my lips and lead a life of gratitude. I will bless the Lord at all times His praise will continually be on my lips.

I see God in everything. I have tasted His grace and goodness and my soul will be forever satisfied in God. I honor the sacredness of prayer and go before my God reverently and with purity of heart, seeking His desire and will for my life.

I know the voice of God because I listen intently for Him. I love to fellowship with my Father I speak to Him about everything.

I enjoy the presence of God, and it is here that I find constant peace and fullness of joy.

I am forever graced and strengthened by Him. Because of this, I can push powerfully beyond the trials to my higher calling through birthing my divine fruit.

I am a fruitful woman because I am in God's presence - always."

Powerful Actions and Reflections

POWERFUL ACTION

Create a list of your influences; the people, places, and things that have a significant impact on your mindset.

Determine if these influences help to magnify the presence of God around you.

Do they lead and support you to seek God through his word and prayer?

If not, make a commitment to remove yourself from these influences and use the time previously invested with them to dwell in the scriptures and prayer.

Personalize Psalm 23 into a prayer. Include your name wherever necessary. Write this prayer and say it three times in succession.

You may also want to consider adding this as part of your daily prayer routine.

POWERFUL REFLECTION

PUSH Principle 3: POWERFUL PRESENCE

How has this PUSH principle fortified your mindset for divine birthing?

What truths about yourself, your influence, and your divine fruit were introduced to you here?

How will you use this principle to step into a divine partnership with God?

Has the principle made you more confident about your ability to fight through difficulties and emerge fruitfully?

What reservations do you have?

WRITE YOUR THOUGHTS AND TAKEAWAYS HERE

YOUR PUSH POWER

 You have a **GREAT POWER** in the presence of the Holy Spirit which is with you always.

 You have a new **TRANSFORMED LIFE** in the Word.

 You **PROSPER** when you obey precepts.

 You have **PROMISES** that are particular to you.

 You discern **GOD'S VOICE** through constant prayer.

 Your praise in the pain **ATTRACTS HEAVEN**.

 You can be *EMPOWERED* by people that honor the presence of the Holy Spirit.

PUSH PRINCIPLE
FOUR

POWERFUL
Perspective

CHAPTER 16

Out Of My Control

Having the right perspective is pivotal to being able to stay steadfast in the storms of life so that you may push powerfully past them and birth your divine fruit. Mindset is so important. Proverbs 23:7 states *"for as he thinketh in his heart, so is he."* You have got to know that everything you face will work for the good purposes of God.

There are so many times when we as humans try to control the narratives of our lives. We are disappointed by the fact that life and the circumstances around us are not shaping up to what we believe they should be. We often find ourselves stubbornly tugging at our situations to force them into the mold that we want them to fit in. Unfortunately, this only leaves us deeply frustrated.

It reminds me of one of the most embarrassing situations of my life. I had just left my home country to take residence in another country to further my education. While I was extremely excited for the new experience, I was also looking forward to the return home for the Christmas holidays.

In the days leading to my return home, I found out that I would not be returning to school for the upcoming semester as the course requirements for that term mandated work experience which I opted to complete at home. This meant that the dorm room, that I had just fabulously outfitted, had to be packed up and stored away in a very short space of time. This proved to be a mighty task as storage was difficult to find.

I did not sleep the night before my early morning departure as I had a whole lot of packing to do. It was also finals week and studying for exams made sleep quite the luxury this week. I was running on fumes and heavily loaded with luggage, as many things had to return with me due to lack of storage.

I got checked in at the airport and as I proceeded toward the departure gate, I was approached by a set of escalators. A very weary me decided to hop on the one of *my choice* with the intent for it to carry me to the next level where my departure gate was located.

Two carry-on bags in hand and one carry-on pulley I jumped on the escalator, and it brought me right back down. *How could this be?* Intent on going up, I pulled my carry-on bag aggressively and was back on the escalator. Again, it forced me right back down.

At this point, I am annoyed and completely frustrated with this thing because I am heavily loaded, and completely exhausted, it's the wee hours of the morning and I just need to catch this flight! Here I go for the third attempt, mustering the bit of strength left in me, and it gave me the same result.

I couldn't help but think that this escalator was being very facetious and wanted to challenge me as I was swiftly ushered back down, yet again. *It was here that it clicked.* I was attempting to go up on the escalator that was designed not to elevate to the higher level but to bring down to the ground level.

I was so focused on what I wanted that I had no regard or respect for the direction the escalator was programmed to operate. I felt like a total fool. Curious and anxious as to whether I had an audience that witnessed this, I turned around slowly, and there they were, a daughter and father just completely astonished at what I attempted to accomplish.

This is what we do in life. We have our minds made up on what should happen; we want to control our realities and each time our expectation is not met; we try again to make it happen irrespective of what life is showing us must happen. We are stubborn about what we want and when we can't get it, we are completely distraught.

We soon come face to face with the realization that situations are not in our control and will not submit to the preferences or timing of our choice. Most times, they are designed to stretch us; so that we can transform into a form necessary to birth our divine fruit. This usually is very difficult to accept because the process is tremendously uncomfortable.

Think about a woman in child birth, it is the labor contractions that work to expand her cervix so that the baby can be released from the womb. Her cervix must transform to facilitate birth. Yes, the contractions are painful but they are necessary in the natural birthing process.

The same applies in divine birthing. The difficulties of life are like contractions, transforming you spiritually and mentally so that you can accommodate the birth of your divine fruit.

Your understanding that you are not in control of this journey of life and where it takes you is critical in remaining powerfully poised for the push. Humility in the journey is necessary.

You must understand that there will be some things that are just out of your control and the only thing you can do in those instances is draw on the comfort and strength of God through trusting Him. It is your enduring and patient response to the uncontrollable that activates your power to push and emerge fruitfully.

When we consider the story of Job (as detailed in the Old Testament book of Job), he was a righteous man and yet still he faced and endured what we may consider unjustifiable circumstances. To a reasonable person, the loss that he endured made no sense for a man who was perfectly aligned with God. The same could be said of Joseph, he was a man who walked uprightly, but he found himself unjustly enslaved and imprisoned for several years (*Genesis 39-41*).

The commonality of these two great men which made them so powerful in their seasons of despair was their unwavering trust in God. They knew that they did not have control of their very own lives, but they also acknowledged that God was in full control. Job 1:21 states *"the Lord gave, and the Lord hath taken away; blessed be the name of the Lord."* He further asserts *"Though he slay me, yet I will trust in Him"* (Job 13:15).

Both Job and Joseph held a unique understanding that led them to release the desire to be in control of their lives in any manner. They were willing to submit to the Lordship of God, regardless of the outcomes and results.

The Old Testament Book of *Daniel* speaks of three Hebrew boys, Shadrach, Meshach, and Abednego, who were thrown in the fire because they refused to worship the king's idols, were okay with what could possibly be their demise. They stood *"fastened in faith"*.

The scripture, Daniel 3: 16-18 states that *"we are not careful to answer thee in this matter. If it be so, our God whom we serve is able to deliver us from the burning fiery furnace, and he will deliver us out of thine hand, O king. But if not, be it known unto three, O king, that we will not serve thy gods, nor worship the golden image which thou has set up."* They knew the power of their God and were content with *wherever* they were being led by Him because they knew that whatever God allow to happen would be necessary for His good will to be accomplished on the earth. This is full submission and surrender that begets fruitfulness.

Life is going to do its own thing no matter how much we have planned. The beauty in this is your posture. Do you have a *posture of great faith* that will allow you to endure and persist even when things go in the totally opposite direction of what you have envisioned? This is what you need!

A mindset of faith in the sovereignty of God that will allow you to stay in the fight and birth your divine fruit. You understand that no matter what befalls you it has to work for your good; the purposes of God has to prevail – your divine fruit must come forth. There is a calm certainty that you know that the difficulties and chaos of life will serve to usher you into the great will of God; into a space of your fruitfulness.

This is why it is so important to have the right perspective so when life starts to color outside of the lines you won't become frazzled and hopeless. You will hold fast to a faith that has led you to believe that whatever confronts you is purposeful; it is necessary for what God wants to do in your life. It is required to birth your *divine fruit*.

Life is wild, messy, and out of control, a complete rodeo! This is perfectly fine, don't try to pretty it up and put a bow on it. Once we live in alignment with God, we will see the beauty emerge from what appears to be pure chaos. There is no need for perfection when God is factored in because He is the "perfector"!

As life taunts you with a tango, be reminded that its dance floor is only so long and so wide. *There is a limit*! At that point, the sovereignty of God arises for glory; the birth of your divine fruit! Get excited about the glory of your fruitfulness!

Chapter 17
A Bigger Picture

We do not have the full story. We are a part of time; and time sits in eternity. Time is released to us day by day and as time is released a little bit of Heaven's plan is manifested on earth. However, we still are without complete understanding as some part of it is being withheld. We cannot hold the events of a day, week, month, year or even decade in isolation because it does not give us a clear view of the grand scheme of things; only God knows this.

In Jeremiah 33:3, the Lord urges *"Call unto me, and I will answer thee, and show thee great and mighty things, which thou knowest not."* The only way to see the big picture is to have it revealed to you by God. This is why Proverbs 3:5-6 reminds us to *"Trust in the Lord with ALL thine heart; and lean not unto thine own understanding. In all thy ways acknowledge him, and he shall direct thy paths"*

It's much like having a thousand-piece puzzle and being given a piece of the puzzle everyday but not seeing how that piece fits in the final product. So, you are not given a full picture of how the completed puzzle should look. If this is the case, you are in no position to understand the fullness of the plan of God and therefore in no position to make an informed move without consulting God.

This is why it is important not to make your current situation the tone of your life because it does not stand alone, it is only a piece of a bigger puzzle. When all the pieces come together, they create a beautiful piece of art, which can finally be well understood but, this revelation comes with time.

There is a basic understanding among powerfully poised women that everything that happens in their journey of life whether good or bad, big or small, is all purposeful and intentionally designed by God.

This is the frame of thought that should always be applied to disappointing situations. You must acknowledge the fact that you have no capacity to fully understand the chaos before you, given the fact that you are a human creature bound by time. However, when you affirm God as the Lord of your life, there is a confidence that builds from your trust in Him that begs you to believe that it all makes perfect sense.

So, cast your fears and cares at the feet of God! Your fears and cares are the birth child of your limited understanding. Release your anxieties knowing based on Romans 8:28 that *"...we know that all things work together for good to them that love God, to them who are the called according to his purpose."*

Every hill and every valley are necessary for the plan of God over your life, and none of them are to be discounted. Each brings value to the place where God wants to carry you; you just need to trust God with it.

There are many of life's experiences that may seem minute but remain powerfully embedded in who you are. I attended a funeral some years ago of a little boy whose death was sudden and tore the hearts of his family wide open.

As I approached the church door to enter the celebration of his life, I could see his eldest brother standing in front of it, inconsolable. There with him, was a friend of the family; a woman considered strong in her faith, and she spoke a few simple words to him that have stuck with me years after. She said, *"Don't try to understand it."* As I walked past, just at the right moment to hear this, I had the revelation that this was the most powerful wisdom one could offer during a time like this.

You do not have the capacity to understand all of life's events. I want to impress on you today, do not try to understand all of life's trials and tribulations, just trust God with them. Trust is imperative for an effective partnership with God. When the bigger picture has yet to be revealed to you and things just don't make sense, your answer is always to trust in the Lord wholeheartedly!

If we had the privilege to plot our own lives, we all would gladly omit every trouble in our path and our days would be sunny and filled with chirping birds and blooming flowers.

We are a pain-averse people. We do not like to experience disruptions, and understandably so. However, it is in the puzzle pieces that are filled with discomfort that our lives find meaning. It is there that we come into our fruitfulness. These pieces are not meant to be understood alone, but are to be connected with other pieces so that the beauty of the bigger picture unfolds.

The power of knowing this and believing it, will evoke a stamina in you to push beyond the difficulties onto the next puzzle piece so that the bigger beautiful picture of your fruitfulness will emerge.

The Kingdom of God needs the full picture of your fruitfulness for its good advancement. Every single one of your life's events (the good, the bad, and the ugly) that contributes to attaining the full picture of your fruitfulness is necessary and very important. It should not be discounted and it should not be considered in isolation.

It is a part of a bigger picture; ZOOM OUT!

CHAPTER 18
Stronger, Wiser, Closer

James 1:2-4 states *"count it all joy when ye fall into divers temptations; knowing this, that the trying of your faith worketh patience. But let patience have her perfect work, that ye may be perfect and entire, wanting nothing."*

We know that everything that happens to us is purposeful and ultimately full of good intent as designed by God. We know that one of the reasons trials come is to make us stronger through increased faith and trust in God.

As we try to seek God for understanding and the way to move ahead, we are strengthened in the knowledge of who He is. God, moved by our diligent search for Him, opens us up to His bountiful wisdom.

Leading an authoritative life requires a strong and hopeful mind. We are not just born with this, but rather this is a state of mind that is acquired with time and experience. It is a mindset that is developed as we continuously emerge from cycles of struggles and disappointments that led us to strengthen our faith in God.

You've heard the saying *"What doesn't kill you makes you stronger"* and that's just the thought here. You are to walk into the valleys of life knowing that you are going to come out stronger in your faith, and therefore will be closer to God. We are not going to wait until the end of this chapter; I want you to affirm with me now *"Stronger! Stronger! Closer! Closer!"*

I can clearly remember a particular time in my life where God was calling, and leading me, to walk through a valley. Yes, a valley! He wasn't leading me not into a place of pleasure, but I was going with my eyes wide open into something that I knew would be painful. Fear struck me! My first thoughts were that this could not be God. He is too great of God to lead me into a space that clearly presents a form of pain for me.

As I made the decision to step away from it, which I considered a move of wisdom, I constantly felt God urging me to walk forward, through this valley! *But why Lord? Don't you know that this will hurt?* Don't you know that this will go against everything you would ever want for me? You want good things for your children, don't you? And the answer I constantly heard was "*Walk!*"

I walked. Reluctantly, *I walked.* Kicking and screaming, *I walked.* I really did not want to face the pain and trauma of it all, I wasn't ready. I had just separated from my husband and that left me depleted in every which way, I had no more left within me.

But I made the decision to be obedient and walk into a situation, I knew from ground zero, from the very beginning, would make me uncomfortable. I knew I would have to stay close to God. I knew I would have to trust Him for this one; and that I did.

I endured that experience for a few years and understood nothing about it as I walked it. But this I do know; it forced me to a point of spiritual *elevation and evolution.* My relationship with God was at a level it had never been in my life! I connected in a way to the Holy Spirit that left even me astonished and amazed many days.

You are reading this book today because of that very same valley experience. This is one of the many plans of Heaven that was birthed out of that pain- *talk about emerging fruitfully!*

Most notably, the renewal of my mind that occurred during that experience prepared me to cope with the death of my mother and grandmother which happened during that time. *I will never doubt God! He is strategic and purposeful!* I call him *Master Orchestrator*!

This is why stepping into a *dynamic divine partnership with God* is so worthwhile and profitable. He lines it all up for optimal impact! Had I not endured that valley for those years, I would not be in good form to impart a message of hope to you, but God knew what I did not!

Though I was reluctant at the onset, I am so happy I decided to trust Him entirely with my steps! Certainly, God leads us in the paths of fruitfulness for His name's sake. It may not always look good but you have got to believe that if you are following God you are walking into the place of your divine fruitfulness.

I share this to say, you can never ever fathom the ways that God will work in your life. He will use something that may seem destructive to you, in the natural, to usher you into unseen levels spiritually.

Isaiah 55: 8-9 states it well, *"For my thoughts are not your thoughts, neither are your ways my ways, saith the Lord. For as the heavens are higher than the earth, so are my ways higher than your ways, and my thoughts than your thoughts."*

Perspective is everything! You have to know that seasons of despair are meant to build you spiritually to elevate you to a new dimension of yourself- this is a fruitful transformation. God also wants to reveal more of himself to you.

You can change how you feel about your situation by simply changing how you think about it. Consider the way you think about the difficulties and challenges you are faced with right now. I challenge you to put a new perspective on it, one that is grounded in purpose.

A valley experience is always an opportunity to soar to new spiritual levels. It prompts you to build an intimate, deep, relationship with God that affords you a faith that exudes unusual strength.

With this strength, you are able to push powerfully through every hindering block, simply because you chose to respond to the pain by drawing closer to God. This is the type of renewed thinking that will induce a great transformation. A renewed thinking that is fruitful and will produce a plentiful harvest.

The humility of drawing close to God and submitting to the opportunity for transformation presented by pain is a powerful act. It eases the burden and brings comfort. You are in a mind space where you can be a teachable student open to the wisdom of Heaven.

God is with you all the way; you just have to embrace Him. Do not resort to trying to fix the pain or praying it away. Face it by submitting it to God. Carry the difficulty to Him and allow Him to walk you through it. Let Him show you how it is intended to grow and strengthen your faith and ultimately usher you into fruitful transformation.

This is the time where you learn the powerful discipline of offering yourself fully to God. This comes with the understanding that only He can usher you out of the maze of pain victoriously. There is an extraordinary version of you on the other side of this, and that fruitful version of you *is stronger, wiser, and closer*!

It is that simple! God wants to use the troubles of life to evoke the emergence of a more powerful, fruitful you. He wants you to bear an unwavering trust in Him and be close enough to him to accurately discern His voice.

The way He chooses to do this is to lead you into valleys where He walks with you, *hand in hand*, and shows you that you can trust Him wholeheartedly. Let's not forget Psalms 23:4 which says, *"Yea, though I walk through the valley of the shadow of death, I will fear no evil: for thou art with me; thy rod and thy staff they comfort me."*

Prior to that valley experience I shared, I prayed that God would put people in my life to help me grow.

When I prayed that prayer, I expected God to surround me with great people of faith, people who were outstanding mentors that I could follow and emulate. But again, His thoughts and ways are so much higher than ours. He placed me in an intimate space with imperfect, lost, and confused folks just like myself and that prompted me to rise up and push to a new level spiritually, in an effort to become untangled and renewed.

He's calling you to do the same. *Woman, arise!* Answer this great call. The pain is calling you closer to God. It is compelling you into the presence of God so that you can transform into the state necessary to birth your divine fruit. It is impossible to be in the presence of God remain in your same old state. When you share space with God fruitful transformation is inevitable- you will show up as new creature.

God's ways are sometimes far from what we imagine they would be, but He only wants to see you stronger than you were before and closer to Him! He's calling you closer, *do you hear him*?

Chapter 19

A Necessary Sacrifice

You are being called to serve! This is the bottom line. The struggles facing you are pointing you to Kingdom service. God is making you suitable for His service. The disruptions in your life are a training ground to build your faith. Often times, God calls you to growth by burdening you with the pain that you are designed to free others from. You are a light to another stricken brother or sister signifying that there is a way out, that there is hope. The cup of suffering that you bear, qualifies you to do just that.

I realized that the pain qualified me for service when I found myself crying uncontrollably on my bedside asking God how my marriage and my life became so frazzled. This was definitely not part of my plan. I made a lot of huge mistakes along the way, including infidelity, which tore me apart. This was not me; this was not what I wanted to do, but somehow, I found myself here in this most imperfect situation. *Why God? How God?* I need an answer. In my crying out, God answered clearly and said, *"This is your cup of suffering."*

I really didn't understand this, and it took me a while to see what God was trying to communicate to me. I knew that Jesus had a cup of suffering and He too asked for it to be taken away. But He stood wholly committed to the cause for the salvation of others which was His honorable service to the world. He offered himself as a sacrifice. Was God telling me that this failing marriage was my sacrifice?

My revelation at that point was that I needed to endure this to be able to serve a people; my people. Those women entrusted to me by God. I was appointed to speak a word of hope to them, so that they would know they too can push powerfully, through every affliction, and emerge anew- phenomenally fruitful. *That woman is you! I am committed to you!*

I want you to see how powerful you are in the midst of the chaos that life presents to you. At the heart of you is a powerful overcomer. You just need to be "activated"! Now, is the time for you to live authoritatively, no matter the season you are in. Don't mind the mess, don't allow it to be a distraction. Use it constructively and allow it to push you to unearth the power than lies deeply within you. Let it be the conduit by which you birth your *divine fruit*.

When you understand that the disruptions you face are necessary to your evolution and your Kingdom service, you will push powerfully pass them to ensure you arrive at a place where your *divine fruit* is fully manifested. You are not pushing just for you, but you push knowing that you are bearing the torch to lead the masses to a great emergence. This is the *power of perspective* you need. The right perspective will shift your attitude and your actions! The right perspective will push you to fruitfulness.

God's intention for you is to be a *faithful servant*. This is made abundantly clear in the second greatest commandment as detailed in Mark 12:31, and that is to *love thy neighbor as thyself.* Your neighbor in this regard can be the people that you are called to help heal and encourage. Your service to them, by way of *your divine fruit*, is your display of love.

The scripture of 1 Thessalonians 5:11 states *"Wherefore comfort yourselves together, and edify one another, even as also ye do."* Each of us is yet only a part of the entire body. However, our parts are all very important as it is linked to the well-being of another. Every test and trial that we face in life makes us fit, and keeps us fit, to serve at our optimum level. For every powerful push we are deepening our roots of faith and birthing our divine fruit which is our honorable service in the Kingdom of God.

If you are anything like me, you've asked God "Why?" many times. I am no stranger to "why fits". Eight billion people on earth and God has chosen you to bear a particular burden. *Your burden is special.* It is your sacrifice which qualifies you as deliverer for a particular people. They need you- don't keep them waiting. Though a heavy burden to bear, the fulfillment of seeing the glory of God manifested in the earth through you, is incomparable! Don't take this pain personal, *it is truly not about you! It's for a bigger purpose!* People are praying to God right now, asking him to send a light, to illuminate their dark path. I am here to tell you that you are that light! *Sister, you are light!* Greater works are your portion! John 14:12-13 states *"Verily, verily, I say unto you, He that believeth on me, the works that I do shall he do also; and <u>greater works than these shall he do</u>; because I go unto my Father. And whatsoever ye shall ask in my name, that will I do, that the Father may be glorified in the Son."* This "greater works" will come in the form of your divine fruit.

Are you going to claim your greater works for the glory of God to arise on the earth? Are you willing to be adamant about emerging fruitfully to serve your people? D.L. Moody, great American evangelist of the 18th century asserts, and I hold firmly to this, *"The world has yet to see what God could do with a man fully consecrated to him. By God's help I aim to be that man!"*

I have vowed to be this woman! I have vowed to be fruitful! You can join me! The world has yet to see how God will use you! Get excited, the works of God are always phenomenal! Birth every divine fruit God has attached to your name. Commit to *fruitful leadership* through a *dynamic divine partnership with God.* Offer your life as a living sacrifice, for the use of the Kingdom of God and watch as he enlarges your territory, your influence, and your impact.

Woman, you are powerful! However, you will only come to live in your true power when you give God *full* control to direct your path. *Will the world be impacted by your divine authority? Will the world taste of your divine fruit?* Please do not deny us of the beauty of you! We await you. We await the illumination of your light and the refreshment of your *divine fruit.*

Chapter 20
I Have The Right Perspective

Remember that as a man thinketh so is he. It is critical that you are living in the right perspective. We are not privy to the full details of God's plan and so this leaves us to trust him. It is this unwavering trust that builds for us a default perspective that no matter what we face it is purposeful and it is making us suitable for the Kingdom service that we have been called to. The difficulties are leading us to birth our *divine fruit*.

Good perspective is everything! It shapes your attitude and behavior, and ultimately dictates how powerfully you stand in life. We are after authoritative living as God has commanded us to dominate from the time of our creation. *"Half- stepping"* is not allowed! Bring the full fruit of your creation to the table of life, and serve it *bountifully, boldly, and unapologetically* because God made you to do so!

It's affirmation time. Open your spirit and soul and let it receive the power of the truth of these words:

"The Holy Spirit has full control over my mind and my thoughts. I know the thoughts and ways of God are higher than I can even comprehend. I also know that God is a God of purpose, love, grace, and mercy and whatever He places before me is very well done.

I will trust the Lord with my whole heart. I will use every difficulty and disappointment to prepare me for my honorable Kingdom service. There are a people waiting for me to experience a freedom they have never seen in their life. I refuse to leave them void of that experience. I am the one! I am the one God chose for them, and I will endure whatever is necessary to be made ready to serve them.

I have the audacity today, and every day of my life, to live in the pandemonium of life powerfully, authoritatively, and unapologetically fruitfully because God designed me to do so!"

Powerful Actions and Reflections

POWERFUL ACTION

Make a list of three times in your life when situations went far out of your control.

Consider how these situations actually worked for your good; how they served to lead you- in any small or big way- toward a path of transformation and fruitfulness.

Write a powerful prayer.

Present a scripture about the reward of trials.

Ask God to help you transform your mind to see the beauty of the difficulties before you.

Ask Him to help you fasten your faith in Him so that you push through the trials and serve the purposes of Heaven according to His will.

POWERFUL REFLECTION

PUSH Principle 4: POWERFUL PERSPECTIVE

How has this PUSH principle fortified your mindset for divine birthing?

What truths about yourself, your influence, and your divine fruit were introduced to you here?

How will you use this principle to step into a divine partnership with God?

Has the principle made you more confident about your ability to fight through difficulties and emerge fruitfully?

What reservations do you have?

WRITE YOUR THOUGHTS AND TAKEAWAYS HERE

YOUR PUSH POWER

 Your trials have come to grow your **FAITH**; to mature you spiritually.

 You are here to **SERVE** a people, that await **YOUR LIGHT** in their dark place.

 You have God with you in the valley as you walk, He **COMFORTS** and **STRENGTHENS**.

 You know that everything that confronts you is **PURPOSEFUL**.

# PUSH PRINCIPLE
FIVE

POWERFUL
Patience

Chapter 21
Kairos

When you are absolutely convinced that there is a time that God has appointed for your deliverance and your shift into a space of promise- the *fullness of your fruitfulness*- you do not mind waiting. You will push powerfully until that time because you know it has to come.

There is a time and season for everything. Ecclesiastes 3:11 states *"He hath made everything beautiful in his time."* For every promise that God has revealed to you, there is an appointed time of delivery. Your trials and tribulations are but only for a season after which they must cease. Time is in the ultimate control of God. We don't know exactly when these things will all happen unless God chooses to reveal the details to us. However, we can rest assured that once God said it; it will happen. All we need to do is stay completely anchored in our trust and faith in God.

So many times, we see scriptures stating that God will move, "at the right time", "at the appointed time", "at the fullness of time" or "when the time has come". This suggests to us that the movement of God is planned for a time.

Isaiah 60:22 states *"I the Lord will hasten it in his time."*

Psalm 102:13 states, *"For the time to favour her, yea, the set time, is come."*

Galatians 4:4 *states "But when the fullness of the time was come, God sent forth his Son, made of a woman, made under the law,"*

Habakkuk 2:3 states *"For the vision is yet for an appointed time."*

Everything we go through; every season of our lives has an appointed time attached to it. The call on our lives is to push through, to endure with a *patient power.* Again, because of our limited view, we do not know the appointment time, but based on our life experiences we can attest that God is an on-time God! At some point or the other, we have seen God come to our rescue bringing remedy that shifts our situations in the "nick of time".

As the lyrics of the old and great gospel chorus asserts, *"He may not come when you want him, but He'll be there right on time."* Again, a steadfast trust in God is required to wait until the time that He shows up to shift the season. This is exactly the concept of *Kairos.* Kairos is a Greek word which means right, critical, or opportune time or moment. It is the appointed time in the purpose of God. It is God's divine intervention in your life to accelerate or bring to pass some occurrence or event on your behalf. The time when the purposes of God will prevail in your life ushering you into your most fruitful position.

Many times, we may be wondering when God is going to step in and take control. We pray harder, stronger, and longer, in hopes of getting His attention to let him know that trouble is brewing down here. But what we do not realize, in that moment, is that He is very much present and aware. It's just not the right time to make the move. There is a beauty in understanding this. <u>*The presence of trouble does not negate the presence of God*</u>. He is still here with you! We are often so occupied with the despair in our lives that we don't notice that the powerful presence of God is there with us.

We need to become more aware of His presence and command our souls to magnify Him at all times, especially in the valley.

I recall a time when the stress of single motherhood had just taken a toll on me emotionally, mentally, financially and physically. I was just completely overwhelmed and felt like I could not continue. The burden was heavy, and I wanted to know why it seemed like God wasn't doing anything about it. It felt as if I was on the brink of demise with no sign of deliverance in sight. I was doing my part trying to stay in a relationship with God, and positioning myself to faithfully steward the call on my life to carry the great message of fruitfulness to the women of the world.

Moreover, I was making the best effort to be the best mother I could be to four souls who looked to me with confidence. At this point, the only constant help I had in the form of my dear mother was gone. It was a real adjustment, and I had to show up irrespective of the pain of loss and lack. Motherhood is indeed a great joy, but it comes with its challenges and sometimes they are many.

This time, they were many and it appeared to be more than I could handle! I broke down. All my mind could perceive was injustice. I stepped up into God's "office" like an underpaid worker, demanding that my efforts be credited! *Was anyone up there coming to rescue me?* I was doing the best I could under the circumstances, but I was tired, and it was taking everything out of me. I needed help and I needed it now! I was overwhelmed. *Is God sitting and watching this knowing my heart? How could He?* I almost felt betrayed. These are my transparent thoughts which saturated my weary soul. I had to immediately take them captive and hold them against the incorruptible word of God.

I was soon able to calm down and settle into my spirit. Then I had to repent and ask for the forgiveness of God. I understood that everything not only happens for a reason but happens only for a time. I was willing to accept that and endure. It was a bad day for a single mother of four. As I think about Job, his heart was righteous as detailed in the Old Testament scriptures of Job. He sat in what appeared to be unjustifiable turmoil for a time far beyond what he would have preferred. But God knew that his life was not in danger. Job's life was protected; fully covered by Heaven until this time of trial was over. Job pushed powerfully through with a patience that is still admired today, thousands of years later.

There is a call on us to respect the season we are in and that means trusting God with it because it has to pass, at an appointed time, according to the will of Heaven. It cannot last forever. *What if God wants you to push through your current trial for a decade or two? Is your trust thick enough to withstand and endure?* You must trust God and come to a point where you are completely okay with whenever God chooses to move. You must build a faith in God that allows you to patiently await His appointed time.

As you go through your times of trouble, know that they will not last forever. We do not know when it will come to an end, but we have a confidence in the fact that it has to end. There is a time appointed by Heaven for your deliverance. Further, you must know that your deliverance, your time of promise, is connected to the lives of so many others who depend on the fullness of your divine fruit to be properly positioned in their own place of fruitfulness. God is strategic and when he shifts you into another season, you are not the only thing being freed and enlarged, everything attached to you is impacted as well.

As you push powerfully through whatever presents itself as pain, know that there is an end to that trial, and *just keep pushing* powerfully and persistently until the appointed time of the fullness of your promise and fruitfulness arrives.

Chapter 22

No Fast Track

None of us likes pain, especially when it threatens to interrupt a beautiful experience. We all enjoy the happenings of amusement parks; the thrill is enough to last a lifetime.

However, what cuts into the fun of it all, is having to wait in long lines to ride the attractions, especially during peak seasons like summer. Some parks have come up with a fast pass which exempts you from the wait in the sweltering heat, allowing you the opportunity of a near perfect experience.

There is no fast track in the journey of our lives. Just as we are willing to bask in the mountain top experiences, we must be willing to courageously endure the valleys.

Life is a journey with highs and lows, and this is what gives it the punch of power it has to awaken us and continually call us higher into purpose and fruitfulness. This is why having the vision of where God wants to carry you is so important.

This among many other things will be your "why". It will give you the strength to patiently endure and powerfully push through until you emerge fruitfully having purposeful impact in the world.

Your fruitful vision is your confidence! It is the picture of your part in the grand mission to advance the Kingdom of God on earth. You are designed for a *dynamic divine partnership* with God.

Go before God in prayer and seek out your assignment; get the revelation of the picture of your fruitfulness. Pursue God for it tenaciously and relentlessly. Do not leave the throne until He has revealed it to you. If you are to be patient in the chaos, you need to acquire the vision, *know where your Rome is!*

There was a time when I kept dreaming about a close friend of mine. With each dream she was pregnant or had a baby. This lead me to make inquiry of her because I knew she had no desire to expand her family. She confirmed that she was indeed not pregnant.

I went into prayer about this, because the reoccurrence of the dream meant that God had a message for her. In my prayer was the vision that God had for her in full color and intricate detail.

I contacted her about this, giving every detail of what was revealed to me. She confirmed that exactly what I had relayed to her, right down to the colors, was all a dream of her heart. The revelation given to me was full confirmation that it was God-ordained. It was what Heaven wanted to birth through her. It was the picture of her fruitfulness.

Shortly after this happened, she found herself in the lowest valley of her life and one of the things she asked of God was to take her out. I assured her that this was a valley to be endured purposefully. There was something in this valley that she needed for that vision we both clearly saw in all its colors.

I urged her to push through powerfully! God was calling her through the pain to birth her fruitful life; to see this vision he had engraved in her heart come to full fruition in the earth. But to get there she would have to PUSH with power!

I want to encourage you as well, *PUSH*! Just like my friend, God has a colorful fruitful vision for your life. I don't know the particulars of your valley, but I do know that it must be endured, there is no fast track past it.

You must push through the pain of it to birth your fruitful life! You can do it! You were made by God to birth it! Keep pushing! No matter how long the push; endure because the beauty at the end of it will make you forget the pain that preceded it.

Let's be students of the valley! Let it prepare you to birth your fruitful vision. Let it prepare and position you to serve your people. This is your training. This is what qualifies you.

You cannot skip this class, do not ask to be exempted from it. This class is not an elective, it is a prerequisite. It is necessary! It is required for the next level of your journey; your transition to fruitfulness. You must be an astute and enduring student and PUSH through it.

Be patient as it takes the necessary time to mold you into the spiritually and mentally form perfect for the birth of your fruitful life. You are transforming; trust the timing of the process.

Allow God to walk you through it. This will require an ear that is inclined to hear His voice. Get close to him and let him guide you; step by step. Walk in pace with God and not ahead of Him. Each step you take is carefully considered and crafted by God. Just be patient in each step. Don't hurry out; wait on God.

Waiting on God looks like being fully present in today. Not so focused on the future but knowing there is a step that God requires you to take today to get to the great vision of fruitfulness He has shown you.

This requires you to focus intensely on God; to keep your mind fastened on Him. God may just require increased intimacy with you for a time period. In this instance, you may find yourself being isolated from familiar spaces so that He can commune with you on a deeper level through study of the scriptures and prayer.

On the other hand, He may be pushing you into intense action. This means He will use you to serve those around you in some capacity as you are pushing through the pain and difficulties. Yes, you may feel a mess in the chaos of your life but God can very well summon you for service in this state.

There are times when I have to pull myself out of the ravages of single motherhood, battered and bruised, dust myself off for just a moment and ascend a stage to inspire the heart of a room full of people. Those people not even knowing that just moments before I was drying tears of distress. I show up in the mess every time I am called because it is my honorable duty to keep pushing and keep fighting.

So, please understand that "waiting on God" does not exempt you from action. It is not permission to sit and do nothing. As you are patiently waiting for your shift to a place of promise, understand that there is always some action that God is compelling you to no matter the magnitude.

This book you are reading is a call to service in the wait. As I shared with you in the beginning, I am still facing difficulties. I have not seen my shift into promise as yet. But I do know that even though it is hard, I must push to show up while enduring the toughest of times.

You must move your focus away from the discomfort of the despair and focus on your present call to service; the assignment God is calling you to now. The only way to do that is to stay close and *diligently follow the lead of God*.

I was once confounded by the mystery of mazes. One day, I was led to determine the best way to find the way out of them. There are corn mazes set up in various cities around the world that allow you to navigate your way out of them as a fun activity.

As I researched this, I found that the best and easiest way to find your way out of a maze was to place your hand at the right side of the maze *from the start* and let it glide *without moving it*, just following that right hand until you are out.

This blew my mind! *The power of the right hand!* All through the scriptures we see God upholding and delivering His people with His right hand. Life can be a difficult maze at times. But, if we hold onto the powerful right hand of Jesus and follow Him through, He will uphold us as the scriptures promise and lead us out safely and fruitfully- this is victory! Don't ask God to scoop you out of it, He is right there with you.

Will you walk patiently with Him?

Will you take His right hand as you wait?

CHAPTER 23

Peace In The Wait

The beauty of being patient and waiting on God is that you are given access to a wonderful peace. You are not burdened or pressured to work for an intended result or outcome to occur because you know that it is in the capable hand of God. You become adorned with peace all because you have chosen to trust God with the turnout and the timing.

So many times, I found myself discouraged in a crumbling marriage trying to make sense of it all. *How do I fix this? Which next step should I take?* With each turn came a new problem that felt like a regression. There were two scriptures God placed in my spirit which encouraged me during that time, and I always carry them with me: Galatians 6:9 *"Let us not be weary in well doing: for in due season we shall reap, if we faint not."* and Psalm 27:14 *"Wait on the Lord: be of good courage, and He shall strengthen thine heart."*

Both of these scriptures held true. God was able to give my heart a peace that would transcend all understanding. This is the peace that would help me through the most difficult times in my life. I know what it is to have peace in the midst of complete despair. My greatest experience of peace was in the time when I faced the loss of my mother. This was a peculiar and disastrous season. I was a newly separated single mother of four young children. I had one true support through this; my mother. She was now gone. Peace should not have been my portion.

Sometimes we have moments where we can relate to how Jesus felt on the cross during his ninth hour. When he cried out and asked, *"My God, my God, why hast thou forsaken me?"* (Matthew 27:46). Though we do not and will not ever face a feat equal to the one that Jesus did, our troubles allow us to connect with His experience at some level.

Oh, but God! In this most vulnerable and seemingly hopeless state where you are stripped of everything, He will give you a peace that's uncommon! Job, Joseph, and Paul knew very well of this peace. Paul says in Philippians 4:11-13, *"For I have learned, in whatsoever state I am, therewith to be content. I know both how to be abased, and I know how to abound: everywhere and in all things, I am instructed both to be full and to be hungry, both to abound and to suffer need. I can do all things through Christ which strengtheneth me."* This contentment which is also freely available to us is the birthchild of peace.

I've always held fast to the fact that the signature of the presence of God is peace. This is my daily and constant goal to ensure that I can lean on God entirely. Total trust in God grants access to the fullness and richness of His presence at which peace is the center. Where there is peace, there is fruitfulness. This is because you are able to be still and maintain a sound communion with God which allows you to follow him as He leads. Without this peace, you are frazzled and misaligned with the steps of God.

There is no greater joy than the comfort of peace as you push through the troubled days of life. In John 16:33, Jesus says *"These things I have spoken unto you, that in me ye might have peace. In the world ye shall have tribulation: but be of good cheer; I have overcome the world*." Peace is evidence that Jesus has indeed conquered.

I want you to understand today that true peace is of God and God alone. This world does not have peace and therefore cannot give it. It can only render things that come under the pretense of peace, but we know that true peace is lasting and non-circumstantial. Nothing in this world can diminish it or take it away.

The beauty of peace is *available* to you right now, wherever you are, at this very moment. It simply requires that you submit every fear, anxiety, and worry to God and make the conscious decision to wait on Him. Peace is evidence of your confidence in God to render the right remedy at the right time. Peace is a sign that you are in a dynamic divine partnership with God. You can push through powerfully when you have the peace of God. Psalms 46:10 says, "*Be still, and know that I am God*". There is strength in your stillness; your ability to trust God enough to wait on His next move. There is freedom and fruitfulness in your patience.

Peace requires you to release. It requires you to cast your care before the throne of God. Imagine that you had a helium-filled balloon attached to a string in your hand right now. If you are in the open air with this balloon the only way for you to secure that balloon is to continue holding it tightly by the string to avoid it slipping away.

As a mother, I know about guarding helium-filled balloons with my life. My balloon grip is like none other. We hold on to our problems as if we are holding on to a helium-filled balloon in the open air. We are afraid to let go, afraid to let it out of our sight and control. I am here to tell you today to release it! Let that balloon fly high into the heavens. Usher each and every one of your problems to your good and very capable God! As you do this, forgive anyone of any offenses, and hold on to nothing! Just like that, with that simple release, you have invited peace into your life. You have gotten rid of the blocks to your fruitfulness. *You can breathe easy now.* You've given your problems over to the one that specializes in the management and orchestration of your life and ultimately your fruitfulness.

Welcome God's peace. 1 Peter 5:7 says, *"Casting all your care upon him; for he careth for you."* Let's take action to symbolize the release of our cares so peace, freedom, and fruitfulness can reside with us. I want to challenge you to release a balloon into the heavens as a sign that you've surrendered it all. On that balloon, write "To: God, from: (Insert Your Name)", then write your greatest worries and end by saying "Thank you." As you release it, whisper "Father, I surrender it all to you. I will wait for you." You've now released it all under the care of the Sovereign Lord. *Congratulations, you are free!*

Philippians 4:6-7 states *"Be careful for nothing, but in everything by prayer and supplication with thanksgiving let your request be made known unto God. And the peace of God, which passeth all understanding, shall keep your hearts and minds through Christ Jesus."* Peace is your portion. God's peace is your path to true freedom. True freedom creates a clear way for fruitfulness. May His peace forever abide with you as you prosper and bear your divine fruit.

CHAPTER 24

A Righteous Reward

Patience is a virtue that brings a righteous reward. We know that our patience ultimately leads to promise. Job asserted his confidence in this when, he said *"But he knoweth the way that I take: when he hath tried me, I shall come forth as gold."* (Job 23:10)This held true as he was restored double. Sometimes God gives us signs of the time that the promise will come. This becomes your hope and encourages your patience. We all recall the story of the birth of Jesus, the wise men were guided by the star. The star was the sign that the promise had come to earth.

Getting to the promise- *the fullness of your fruitfulness*- is a most thrilling experience. Here it is, you can see the vision in real time. You can literally touch the *fruit of your faith*! While this is great, I do believe that the person you would have evolved into on the way to the promise is an even greater reward. You would have pushed powerfully through the pain and difficulties and emerged with divine fruit that last. You cannot be in full and passionate pursuit of fruitfulness and stay the same; you will change. *You will become stronger, closer, wiser, and more fastened in faith!* You will become an *extraordinary* version of yourself. You would have walked further into the truth of you; deeper into your divine authority- your place of fullness and fruitfulness.

This evolution was necessary. You had to become the person fit for the promise. You are now renewed by the transformation of your mind which is now firmly grounded in *faith in God*. You have become fit to enter the promise. It is the change in your mindset that has elevated you to the door of promise and fruitfulness. You have proven yourself faithful and steadfast; an excellent and effective *partner of God*.

The miracle is really in the change of you. You have become powerfully postured by your patience. You are in a space and place where you have grown in the Spirit. You have eyes that see and ears that hear. You are sensitive to the word of Heaven and the voice of God. You are at the place where you a pliable enough to receive and respond to God. God can use you. He knows that His will matters most to you. Like the Lord said about David, whom He favored, *"I have found David, the son of Jesse, a man after mine own heart, which shall fulfill all my will."* (Acts 13:22) The *"new and fruitful you"* is a woman relentlessly after the heart and will of God.

It is your faithfulness that attracts the favor of God. Psalm 84:11 tells us that *"no good thing will He withhold from them that walk uprightly."* As you walk with the Lord you are transformed. This transformation will be so phenomenal that even you will be astonished by how God has brought you to an uncommon evolution. He will lead you step by step into His perfect design for you. God wants to bring you out of this valley victoriously and fruitfully. Like Job you may be stripped; like Joseph you may be isolated, but you must be willing to trust him and wait on His deliverance. Wait for your righteous reward which will come at God's appointed time.

You may lose those things that are nearest and dearest to your heart. Your family, your possessions, your job, and your health, but he wants you to remain trusting in Him that He will make all things work for good. He will make it happen. His intervention will free you from the despair, that desired only to stifle you, so that the beauty of your creation- *your fruitfulness*- can spring forth.

Restoration and Resurrection are in order! Did you hear me? I said restoration and resurrection are in order! The real power of you is your ability to *"die"* to a thing and resurrect renewed through Jesus Christ. When you have resurrected you have entered a new dimension of you. Job's restoration was double. Everything he lost was restored to him twice more. This is a new level. This is the beauty in waiting on God, he does all things better than we can ever do it! Psalms 34:5 states *"they looked unto him and were lightened: and their faces were not ashamed."* This is the truth. At the right time, you will come forth with a radiance that cannot be denied. This is victory afforded by your willingness to step into fruitfulness.

The fruition of an earthly promise is most satisfying, but even more fulfilling is the promise of the eternal glory of heaven. As Paul has said *"I press toward the mark for the prize of the high calling of God in Christ Jesus."* (Philippians 3:14) This is the righteous reward that tops anything we can ever see manifested on this earth. If we find that we have no hope at all we can look to a higher hope, an eternal hope of the promise of being called into the heavenly kingdom. If there is anything worthy of the wait, it is the joy of being called to the heavenly home. It is knowing that your name is written in Heaven as a partner of God affords a great peace.

Do not let your eyes fool you. Many times, what we see and experience in the natural, attempts to negate the promises and great visions which God has revealed to us. Don't let it! Hold fast to what God has told you. Make sure that your trust is thick enough to endure the trying times until the appointed time of promise has come. You will emerge anew and phenomenally fruitful when your trust meets *Kairos*, your time of promise. Your trust is therefore the only thing under your control, don't drop it! Fasten your faith and see your *divine fruit* emerge!

Hebrews 12:2 states *"Looking unto Jesus the author and finisher of our faith, who for the joy that was set before him endured the cross, despising the shame, and is set down at the right hand of the throne of God."* The joy of Heaven is enough for me. I will push powerfully even if it means that the only reward I see is on the other side, because that is truly the only just reward.

My patience is grounded not only in my hope of the manifestation of earthly promises at their appointed time but also in my hope of the eternal glory of Heaven. There is no better reward. The only way to both of these is a relentless commitment to your fruitfulness.

Heaven is calling you; *Woman PUSH powerfully!*

Chapter 25

I Have The Patience To Endure!

You are powerfully poised for the push when you don't mind waiting! You have a peace about you because your mind is set on Christ and His ability to deliver you from every affliction and usher you into promise- *a place of fruitfulness.*

You know the kind of God that you serve, and you believe like King David asserted in 1 Chronicles 19:13 (KJV), *"Let the Lord do that which is good in his sight!"* You can have peace because you know that you are in *divine partnership* with a fair and just God.

You know the reward will be righteous. While you are looking onward to the earthly promises being manifested, you are even more hopeful to witness and experience the glory of Heaven.

This is the eternal hope you patiently await. This gives you the most peace.

You've got to believe that there is a beauty in waiting. It is in your waiting period that you are positioned for the promise. You come out of the waiting a *new* version of yourself.

Everything that truly fulfills comes out of your season of patient waiting. Your wait presents the opportunity for you to experience peace at its purest. Moreover, it positions you for the fullness of your fruitfulness.

Let's affirm together:

"I am powerfully equipped for the life that God has prepared for me. The hills and the valleys; I am prepared to enjoy and endure them all.

I know that God is with me, right here. Because I trust God fully with my life, I have a peace that passes every understanding.

I know that God is going to bring me out of this victoriously. I will receive my righteous reward. I am excited about the victory of being renewed and evolved in the spirit.

I will be an extraordinary fruitful version of who I am today. Above anything else, I look forward to the eternal glory of heaven which awaits me.

I am strong because I honour stillness. I am powerful because I can wait patiently in the pit until the time that God so chooses to deliver me by the manifestation of the promise.

This promise is the great vision of God over my life and it bears the fullness of my fruitfulness.

I submit patiently and completely to the will, way, and wonderful works of God all the days of my life."

Powerful Actions and Reflections

POWERFUL ACTION

Make a focus statement. This is the declaration you will make every time you notice that your thoughts are moving away from God and the ultimate vision He has given you.

When you get weary in the waiting this statement that will quicken your spirit and call your thoughts back into alignment with the will of God over your life.

It should strengthen you as you continue to wait on God to transition you into your place of promise.

Write a powerful prayer. Present a scripture in prayer that speaks to the fact that time is under the sovereign rule of heaven.

Ask God to increase your faith so that you can develop a steady posture of patience to wait for his appointed time.

POWERFUL REFLECTION

PUSH Principle 5: POWERFUL PATIENCE

How has this PUSH principle fortified your mindset for divine birthing?

What truths about yourself, your influence, and your divine fruit were introduced to you here?

How will you use this principle to step into a divine partnership with God?

Has the principle made you more confident about your ability to fight through difficulties and emerge fruitfully?

What reservations do you have?

WRITE YOUR THOUGHTS AND TAKEAWAYS HERE

YOUR PUSH POWER

 Your **PEACE** comes from your **PATIENCE**;

 Your **PROMISE** has an appointed time;

 Your **STRENGTH** is in your stillness & submission to the steps & timing of God;

 Your valley prepares you for the **PROMISE**.

Epilogue

> *"And God blessed them, and God said unto them, Be fruitful, and multiply, and replenish the earth, and subdue it."* Genesis 1:28

The bottom line is you were created to rule, according to your creative design.

This book is a call to live an authoritative life as a *fruitful woman*. If you master the five *PUSH principles*, you will build a faith that will fortify your mind so that you can push resiliently through a troubled life and emerge fruitfully. Your *faith* allows for fortitude through *divine partnership* with God which ushers you to *fruitfulness*.

God is most interested in your divine fruit because it is the manner which you are called to serve your people on the earth. It is your unique influence that I refer to as your *fruitful leadership*. The works of the Kingdom of God will advance only if you are determined and diligent about birthing your divine fruits for the enrichment of the people in your sphere.

You cannot create fruitfulness on your own. Fruitfulness comes through remaining in Jesus Christ by faith. This is why a *divine dynamic partnership with God* is entirely necessary if you are to live a fruitful life.

The great apostle of the New Testament Paul, knew this all too well. Paul tells us that all things are possible through Christ who gives us strength (Philippians 4:13). Let me be very clear about it, you will need a supernatural strength if you are to be fruitful. This is a strength that can only be afforded by *divine partnership* with God through His son Jesus Christ.

As a woman, your fruitfulness is in your power to *cultivate and keep* every person and thing entrusted to your *"womb"* which is your sphere of influence. The activation of this authority requires a relationship with God which is formed through belief in his son Jesus Christ.

It is by your faith that you become a powerful child of God. John 1:12 states *"But as many as received him, to them gave the power to become the sons of God, even to them that believe on his name"* This is your first step to becoming a fruitful woman, accepting the salvation of God through his son Jesus Christ.

If you have yet to offer God a place in your life, I want to graciously extend to you the offer of salvation. I hope that you will accept. In Jesus, there is fullness of joy and eternal life. I do not want you to miss the abundance available to you by accepting God as your personal savior and Father through Jesus Christ his son.

Romans 10:9-10 states "That if thou shalt confess with thy mouth the Lord Jesus, and shalt believe in thine heart that God hath raised him from the dead, thou shalt be saved. For with the heart, man believeth unto righteousness; and with the mouth, confession is made unto salvation."

If you are ready to accept salvation say this prayer *"Father, I thank you for your love toward me. I believe that you love me so much that you sent your only son Jesus to save my soul. I believe that I will have the fullness of life through your son Jesus Christ. Forgive me of my sins and create in me a clean heart. Restore me so that I live according to your original design and lead me into the path of fruitfulness for your Kingdom's sake. Amen."*

You have now officially entered the service of the Kingdom of God as WOMAN- *"Heaven sent helper"*.

Once you have come to transform your life by connecting with your authenticity and divine identity, you can stand confidently to lead in your sphere of influence.

Every woman, irrespective of her ability to carry and/or care for a child in the natural is being called to mother. God has set you apart to birth, keep, and nurture spiritual visions. Let me remind you that you are pregnant! Yes, right now! Greater works are within you! Your divine fruit is waiting to be birth!

Dwell with the Spirit of God so that he may reveal to you the seeds of visions implanted into your spiritual womb. You have the authority to birth, cultivate, keep, and protect these seeds. Remember it is your seed that will crush the head of the enemy. So be intentional and diligent about birthing your seeds.

You have authority over the environment in which they are planted. You can speak to it, and it must submit to you and align with the visions God gave to you. This is your influence. This is your authority. *This is your Fruitful Leadership*. Live in it!

As you begin to *PUSH* by faith in God, the fruit of your womb will begin to emerge through you piece by piece. Your kingdom duty is to push out the *fullness of your fruit*; so that the full vision of Heaven pertaining to you is manifested on earth.

There is so much power available to you as a woman. You just need to activate your womb to access the entirety of it. You were created and commanded to rule even in the trials and troubles of life! Get in the presence of God, and know who you are as a powerful woman made in His image and likeness. The Kingdom of Heaven needs you now- it needs your fruit!

Become confident about the vision of your womb and be relentless about seeing it happen on earth. Persistently pursue your fruit. Have the audacity to be fruitful in a troubled fickle life. Don't let the strife of life fool you! You are innately powerful. YOU ARE STRONGER THAN THE PAIN.

Defy the odds with your faith in God, *PUSH* and EMERGE WITH YOUR FRUIT- *the harvest of your faith*! This is true authority! This is rulership! This is *Fruitful Leadership*! *You were created for it.*

FRUITFUL WOMAN COME FORTH! *Heaven is waiting for you to PUSH!*

The time is now to show up in your authentic form, powerful, resilient, and fruitful! Step into a dynamic divine partnership with God and watch Him mold you into fruitful form. Once you have embraced your authenticity, become diligent about "feeding" your people with your fruit. You have been sent to their aid and they are waiting to on you. Serve them with excellence even if it means sacrifice. Steward your position of influence well.

WOMAN! PUSH POWERFULLY

As you begin to lead and influence, do not forget to hold fast to the precepts and promises of God. Leverage your prayer and praise, keep the right perspective, and be patient by waiting on God's perfect timing for the fullness of your fruitfulness to emerge! The biggest test will be your patience. Do not get weary and abort the vision and mission toward your fruitfulness. The vision will always hold true.

Habakkuk 2:2-3 encourages us to write the vision down and make it plain. It assures us that the vision is for an appointment time and though it may tarry it will surely come and not delay. You are on your way to great revolution and transformation! You are about to make the earth shake! Get excited! If you saw the full intention of Heaven regarding you, and how *necessary* you are to the *Kingdom of God* you would begin pushing *NOW*!

Woman! It is YOUR time!

Are you ready? Let's go!...

One, two, three...... PUSHHHH!

PUSH *Powerfully*

and

EMERGE *Fruitfully*

Acknowledgments

To my Heavenly Father, thank you for looking past my inadequacies, to which there are still many, and seeing my heart. You have walked with me faithfully every day. I am only here today because you refused to let go of my hand. I am nothing without you. You are a God of integrity and great provision. This book is all you, you made this call clear to me in 2017. Here I stand confidently and courageously to answer that call. All Glory be to You! I Love you wholeheartedly.

To every woman on this earth made in the image and likeness of God, this book is for you. Your Heavenly Father wants you to know, no matter what you are going through, *you are worthy* and valuable to heaven. He just needs you to get closer to Him. The earth needs you to activate your womb now! *It is time to PUSH!* Heaven wants to birth and spring forth the unimaginable from you. Your fruitfulness is important to the Kingdom. God commanded you to live authoritatively when He created you. I urge you; the time is now, live in His presence and *push powerfully*!!! Partner with God to birth your divine fruit in the earth; we need it and we need you. Love you eternally.

To my mother, the late great *Helen Virginia, Barr*, who was the epitome of strength and love. A woman of great wisdom, she ingrained an invaluable virtue of resilience within me that will lead to a powerful impact for generations to come. I am who I am today, because of you. You are still the most powerful influence in my life. You expected me to birth this book. Your belief in me never faltered, you nurtured me unceasingly. You pushed powerfully until your last day. Thank you for mothering me with such devotion. Love you eternally.

To my grandmothers the late *Effie Walkes* and the late *Kathleen Adderley*, you were outstanding women and your impact on my life cannot be denied. It must be credited. The faith I have today is from you both. I know the power of God through his son Jesus because both of you continuously urged me and drew me to His presence. Thank you for your constant prayers which are still alive and active today. Thank you for working effortless to build a foundation for me that does not fail or falter. The baton is now in my hands. I am in the runner's position. As I run, I run with you in mind, knowing that I have been called to further the work you started. I aim to answer that call with diligence and excellency. I vow uphold the great legacy and standard as a faithful mother in the earth. You both were the grandmothers I aspire to be. Thank you for pushing powerfully until the very end! I am a testament of the divine fruit you brought forth in your time. Your living was not in vain. Love you both eternally.

To my daughter *Chloe Summah Bastian* and the twin girls to come, I thank you for inspiring me daily to be my best, to show up as the mother and woman that God has designed me to be. Thank you for seeing past my imperfections and embracing the fullness of love at the center. I want you to have a legacy of faith that cannot be quenched but strong enough to survive for generations far beyond you. That starts with how I live and how I mother you. So, I push powerfully! You are all beautiful women, fearfully and wonderfully made by God. Stay close to God in faith and you will continue to blossom beautifully and push powerfully! I declare that you ae fruitful women of God. Love you eternally.

To my boys, Dawson, Kruiz, Kole and any other great Kings that follow, you've kept me alive and made me so strong. You've given me more of a reason to live authoritatively in this life. You show me grace every single day. May you grow into great good fearing men whose heart are continually postured towards His will. May God use you powerfully. My Kings, it is a privilege and a divine honor to be your Queen Mother. I appreciate you. Love always.

To a great woman of God, the Reverend Angela Palacious. I had the esteem honor of introducing you as keynote speaker at my high school graduation some twenty odd years ago. All those years later, you have been gracious enough to assist me with introducing *Woman Push Powerfully* to the world. I respect the grace on your life and honor you for the great works of your hands during your many years in ministry. You paved the way for women like me to arise in courage and answer the call of God with a spirit of boldness. May God forever bless you Reverend Palacious.

Last but certainly not least, many thanks to my publisher, Universal Impact Press. Aisha and Alicia, your dedication to seeing this book come to fruition is appreciated. It has been long journey but you stayed committed to birthing this fruit alongside me. I can't form into words how important you were to this book. Thank you for walking with me every step away, encouraging, and inspiring. This could not be a reality today without you. Your time and efforts represented in this book is a seed that was sown for a great harvest over many generations to come. I am entirely grateful to God for connecting our paths at such a time as this. Thank you.

About The Author

Krista Barr-Bastian was born and raised in Nassau Bahamas. She is a separated single mother of four beautiful children: Chloe, Dawson, Kruiz and Kole. She has a deep passion for women and seeing them use their *faith* to step into a *dynamic divine partnership* with God to unlock their innate strength and *birth their divine fruits* in the earth for the advancement of the *Kingdom of God*.

Very tenacious, she is no stranger to the strife of life having pushed powerfully through seasons of great loss, to birth the visions and plans of heaven attached to her. *Woman! Push Powerfully** is the first book she has authored. Krista is also the founder of Events *by Krista.* This platform produces transformational experiences and teachings for women, empowering them to emerge out of difficult life altering seasons renewed and fruitful! If you are interested in further teachings or talks on *fruitful living and fruitful leadership* among *women*, you may connect with her on Instagram at @eventsbykrista.

THE *Holiday* EDITION

EXCLUSIVE *Bonuses*

Fruitful Woman Affirmation

I am powerfully poised for fruitfulness. I seek God relentlessly and desire earnestly for His presence.

I am a "Heaven-sent helper" in a dynamic divine partnership with God. My will is aligned with God's will. I am after his purpose for my life continually.

I have a people and I aim to serve them with all of me. I will birth my divine fruit so the lives of the people in my sphere of influence can be enriched and enlarged.

I hold on to the powerful word and promises of God and elevate my praise and prayer no matter where life takes me.

I do not seek to understand because I trust God with my whole heart. I know that whatever I endure is purposeful and intended to draw me closer to God and to make me stronger. I will wait on God. I have the patience to wait because I know He does all things well in the right time; the appointed time. I am at peace with whatever God does. I am focused on the eternal hope which transcends this world. This is the ultimate reward; the glory of heaven. This is the ultimate reward; an eternal hope which transcends this world.

I am fruitful through Christ! I continue to emerge renewed and impactful, allowing heaven to birth its visions through me for the advancement of the Kingdom of God.

I am a FRUITFUL WOMAN in a dynamic divine partnership with God. I will PUSH powerfully all the days of my earthly life to see the good glory of God arise boldly in the earth.

Fruitful Woman Prayer

D^{*ear Heavenly Father,*}

You are the sovereign ruler of the heavens and the earth. There is no one like you Lord!

I thank you for creating me in your image and your likeness. You have called me to show up with authority in this world. I am submitting to you wholeheartedly through dynamic divine partnership with you to answer this call. I am a fruitful woman.

You've created me with great influence to shift and transform the environments that I dwell in. Through you I am more powerful than any pain or pit that seeks to consume me. It will not stop me! I will PUSH powerfully through and emerge victoriously with my divine fruit.

You've implanted heaven's visions in my womb. Reveal the fullness of them to me so that I can use my influence to see them manifested here on earth. I am committed to the vision of my womb Lord. May I be fortified with the strength of mind to push through and powerfully impact the world around me for your Kingdom.

Thank you, Lord, for the anointing and appointment on my life. It is an honor and a privilege to serve you. I am forever your humble and faithful servant. Your "Heaven- sent helper".

I am honoured to be in such a dynamic divine partnership with you. May I live in the awesome fear of you Lord, and in the authority that you graced me with.

May I be fruitfully for your good glory all the days of my life.

In the Powerful Name of Your Son Jesus Christ, Amen.

Fruitful Woman Scriptures

You will manifest the most authentic and fruitful version of yourself when you live in God through a *dynamic divine partnership* with God. The things of this world will never satisfy you. True fulfillment is found in God through Jesus Christ His Son. Get in the will of God and watch the fruit and power of you Emerge!

Below are scriptures that will keep you postured in a fruitful mindset as they enforce the five PUSH principles.

These scriptures will help you maintain the strength of mind you need to PUSH and birth your divine fruit for the advancement of the Kingdom of God in your sphere of influence.

POWERFUL PERSON

"So God created man in his own image, in the image of God created he him; male and female created he them." **GENESIS 1:27**

"And the LORD God said, It is not good that the man should be alone; I will make him a help meet for him" **GENESIS 2:18**

"For thou hast possessed my reins: thou hast covered me in my mother's womb. I will praise thee; for I am fearfully and wonderfully made: marvelous are thy works; and that my soul

knoweth right well. My substance was not hid from thee, when I was made in secret, and curiously wrought in the lowest parts of the earth. Thine eyes did see my substance, yet being unperfect; and in thy book all my members were written, which in continuance were fashioned, when as yet there was none of them." **PSALM 139:13-16**

"But when it pleased God, who separated me from my mother's womb, and called me by his grace, to reveal his Son in me..." **GALATIANS 1:15-16**

"I am crucified with Christ: nevertheless I live; yet not I, but Christ liveth in me: and the life which I now live in the flesh I live by the faith of the Son of God, who loved me, and gave himself for me." **GALATIANS 2:20**

"Strength and honor are her clothing; and she shall rejoice in time to come. She openeth her mouth with wisdom; and in her tongue is the law of kindness". **PROVERBS 31:25-26**

"Favor is deceitful, and beauty is vain: but a woman that feareth the Lord, she shall be praised." **PROVERBS 31:30**

But now thus saith the LORD that created thee, O Jacob, and he that formed thee, O Israel, Fear not: for I have redeemed thee, I have called thee by thy name; thou art mine. **ISAIAH 43:1**

POWERFUL PURPOSE

"Before I formed thee in the belly I knew thee; and before thou camest forth out of the womb I sanctified thee, and I ordained thee a prophet unto the nations." **JEREMIAH 1:5**

"And be not conformed to this world: but be ye transformed by the renewing of your mind, that ye may prove what is that good, and acceptable, and perfect, will of God.". **ROMANS 12:2**

"But seek ye first the kingdom of God, and his righteousness; and all these things shall be added unto you." **MATTHEW 6:33**

"For what shall it profit a man, if he shall gain the whole world, and lose his own soul?" **MARK 8:36**

"Ye are the light of the world. A city that is set on a hill cannot be hid."**MATTHEW 5:14**

"And he said unto them, How is it that ye sought me? wist ye not that I must be about my Father's business?" **LUKE 2:49**

"I must work the works of him that sent me, while it is day: the night cometh, when no man can work" **JOHN 9:4**

"Who knoweth whether thou art come to the kingdom for such a time as this?" **ESTHER 4:14**

"Behold the handmaid of the Lord; be it unto me according to thy word." **LUKE 1:38**

"And blessed is she that believed: for there shall be a performance of those things which were told her from the Lord.". **LUKE 1:45**

"Verily, verily, I say unto you, He that believeth on me, the works that I do shall he do also; and greater works than these shall he do; because I go unto my Father.". **JOHN 14:12**

"Ye have not chosen me, but I have chosen you, and ordained you, that ye should go and bring forth fruit, and that fruit should remain: that whatsoever ye shall ask of the Father in my name, he may give it to you.". **JOHN 15:16**

"Abide in me, and I in you. As the branch cannot bear fruit of itself, except it abide in the vine; no more can ye, except ye abide in me. I am the vine, ye are the branches: He that abideth in me, and I in him, the same bringeth forth much fruit: for without me ye can do nothing. If a man abide not in me, he is cast forth as a branch, and is withered; and men gather then, and cast them into the fire, and they are burned. If ye abide in me, and my words abide in you, ye shall ask what ye will, and it shall be done unto you.' **JOHN 15:4-7**

POWERFUL PRESENCE

"Blessed is the man that walketh not in the counsel of the ungodly, nor standeth in the way of sinners, nor sitteth in the seat of the scornful. But his delight is in the law of the Lord; and in his law doth he meditate day and night. And he shall be like a tree planted by the rivers of water, that bringeth forth his fruit in his season; his leaf also shall not wither; and whatsoever he doeth shall proposer." **PSALM 1: 1-3**

"Thy word is a lamp unto my feet, and a light unto my path". **PSALM 119: 105**

"Man shall not live by bread alone, but by every word that proceedeth out of the mouth of God.' **MATTHEW 4:4**

"It is the spirit that quickeneth; the flesh profiteth nothing: the words that I speak unto you, they are spirit, and they are life." **JOHN 6:63**

"For the word of God is alive and active. Sharper than any double-edged sword.." **HEBREWS 4:12**

"Bless the Lord, *O my soul: and all that is within me, bless his holy name. Bless the* Lord, *O my soul, and forget not all his benefits."* **PSALM 1: 1-3**

"Rejoicing in hope; patient in tribulation; continuing instant in prayer." **ROMANS 12:12**

"I have set the Lord always before me: because he is at my right hand, I shall not be moved." **PSALM 16:8**

"For he shall be as a tree planted by the waters, and that spreadeth out her roots by the river, and shall not see when heat cometh, but her leaf shall be green; and shall not be careful in the year of drought, neither shall cease from yielding fruit." **JEREMIAH 17:8**

"They looked unto him and were lightened: and their faces were not ashamed." **PSALM 34:5**

"Therefore I say unto you, What things soever ye desire, when ye pray, believe that ye receive them, and ye shall have them". **MARK 11:24**

"Pray without ceasing. In everything give thanks: for this is the will of God in Christ Jesus concerning you." **1 THESSALONIANS 5:17-18**

"The effectual fervent prayer of a righteous man availeth much." **JAMES 5:16**

"If ye abide in me, and my words abide in you, ye shall ask what ye will, and it shall be done unto you. Herein is my Father glorified, that ye bear much fruit, so shall ye be my disciples." **JOHN 15:7-8**

"Now the Lord is that Spirit: and where the Spirit of the Lord is, there is liberty. But we all, with open face beholding as in a

glass the glory of the Lord, are changed into the same image from glory to glory, even as by the Spirit of the Lord. **2CORINTHIANS 3:17-18**

POWERFUL PERSPECTIVE

"The steps of a good man are ordered by the Lord: *and he delighteth in his way."* **PSALM 37:23**

"The Lord is my shepherd; I shall not want." **PSALM 23:1**

"There are many devices in a man's heart; nevertheless the counsel of the Lord, that shall stand." **PROVERBS 19:21**

"And we know that all things work together for good to them that love God, to them who are the called according to his purpose." **ROMANS 8:28**

"For my thoughts are not your thoughts, neither are your ways my ways, saith the LORD. For as the heavens are higher than the earth, so are my ways higher than your ways, and my thoughts than your thoughts." **ISAIAH 55:8-9**

"For I know the thoughts that I think toward you, saith the Lord, thoughts of peace, and not of evil, to give you an expected end." **JEREMIAH 29:11**

"Though he slay me, yet will I trust in him" **JOB 13:15**

"But he knoweth the way that I take: when he hath tried me, I shall come forth as gold." **JOB 23:10**

"Beloved, think it not strange concerning the fiery trial, which is to try you, as though some strange thing happened unto you;" **1 PETER 4:12**

"When thou passest through the waters, I will be with thee; and through the rivers, they shall not overflow thee: when thou walkest through the fire, thou shalt not be burned; neither shall the flame kindle upon thee." **ISAIAH 43:2**

"But when Jesus heard it, he answered him, saying, Fear not: believe only, and she shall be made whole." **LUKE 8:50**

POWERFUL PATIENCE

"I the Lord will hasten it in his time." **ISAIAH 60:22**

"He hath made everything beautiful in his time" **ECCLESIASTES 3:11**

"For the vision is yet for an appointed time, but at the end it shall speak, and not lie: though it tarry, wait for it; because it will surely come, it will not tarry." **HABAKKUK 2:3**

"For to be carnally minded is death; but to be spiritually minded is life and peace." **ROMANS 8:6**

"And he said unto her, Daughter, thy faith hath made thee whole; go in peace, and be whole of thy plague." **MARK 5:34**

"And let us not be weary in well doing: for in due season we shall reap, if we faint not." **GALATIANS 6:9**

"Wait on the LORD: be of good courage, and he shall strengthen thine heart: wait, I say, on the LORD." **PSALM 27:14**

"Love not the world, neither the things that are in the world. If any man love the world, the love of the Father is not in him...And the world passeth away, and the lust thereof: but he that doeth the will of God abideth forever." **1 JOHN 2:15, 17**

Made in the USA
Columbia, SC
17 December 2023

28751229R00133